Study Guide for

Deaux, Dane, and Wrightsman's

Social Psychology in the '90s

Sixth Edition

Study Guide for

Deaux, Dane, and Wrightsman's

Social Psychology in the '90s

Sixth Edition

Glenn Littlepage
Middle Tennessee State University

Brooks/Cole Publishing Company
Pacific Grove, California

Brooks/Cole Publishing Company

A Division of Wadsworth, Inc.

Printed in the United States of America
5 4 3 2

ISBN 0-534-10400-2

Sponsoring Editor: *Marianne Taflinger*
Production Editor: *Penelope Sky*
Cover Design: *Roy R. Neuhaus*

CONTENTS

Study Guide for

Deaux, Dane, and Wrightsman's

Social Psychology in the '90s

Sixth Edition

CHAPTER ONE

HISTORY AND SYSTEMS OF SOCIAL BEHAVIOR

CHAPTER OUTLINE

A History of Social Psychology

Theories in Social Psychology

Role Theories

- Basic Assumptions and Concepts
- Contributions to Social Psychology

Learning Theories

- Basic Assumptions and Concepts
- Contributions to Social Psychology

Cognitive Theories

- Basic Assumptions and Concepts
- Contributions to Social Psychology

A Comparison of Perspectives

What Social Psychologists Do

CHAPTER REVIEW

Chapter 1 defines social psychology as the field that explores how our thoughts, feelings, and behavior are influenced by others. Others influence us not only when they are actually present, but by their implied or imagined presence. That is, other people can influence us when we think about their behavior or their possible reactions to us.

The year 1898 is a date that is frequently given for the origin of the field of social psychology. In that year, two influential publications discussed different aspects of social behavior. A few years later, early textbooks, professional journals, and several important studies provided additional contributions to the developing field. During the 1920's 30's and 40's social psychology began to refine its focus, develop its own theoretical basis, and establish a strong emphasis on empirical rigor. Kurt Lewin's field theory, which emphasized that both personal and environmental factors determine social behavior, was a major development in the history of social psychology. The great majority of the knowledge in social psychology has been discovered since World War II. Today, social psychology is an established and dynamic discipline.

Theories are used to organize and clarify our knowledge concerning a topic. Modern social psychology is guided by three major theories: role theory, learning theory, and cognitive theory. Role theory emphasizes that our behavior is greatly influenced by the expectations of others and our positions within a social context. Learning theory emphasizes that much of our social behavior is learned from direct experience, or from observing others. Cognitive theory emphasizes that our behavior depends upon the manner in which we perceive and understand other people. These theories provide different perspectives from which to view social behavior. No one theory has the corner on the whole truth. Rather we can often get a more complete understanding by examining an issue from various theoretical perspectives. The three theories described in this chapter will be applied to specific topics throughout the book.

LEARNING OBJECTIVES

After completing Chapter 1, you should be able to:

1. Describe 2 events that occurred in 1898 that caused some observers to pinpoint that date as the beginning of the field of social psychology. (p. 3)

2. Identify three important contributions of field theory. (p. 5)

3. Describe 3 basic purposes of theories. (p. 6)

4. List and explain 3 necessary characteristics of a good theory. (p. 7)

5. Define role expectations and explain why they are important. (p. 7-8)

6. Explain two types of role conflict. (p. 9)

7. Define and give an example of each of the following concepts: stimulus, response, reinforcement, stimulus generalization, stimulus discrimination. (p. 11)

8. Use concepts from social learning theory to distinguish between learning and performance, and explain the causes of each. (p. 12-13)

9. Construct an outcome matrix (like the one in Figure 1.3) to summarize the patterns of rewards and costs of two individuals (such as a dating couple when one person wants to go to a party and the other one wants to go to the football game). (p. 14)

10. Distinguish between mental processing and mental representation. (p. 15)

11. Describe two major functions that may be served by a schema. (p. 16)

12. Describe the central concept for each of the three major theoretical perspectives of social psychology. (p. 18)

13. Explain which theory most strongly emphasizes the present. (p. 18-19)

14. Explain which theory focuses most closely on internal processes. (p. 18-19)

15. Explain which theory places the greatest emphasis on the social rather than individual causes of behavior. (p. 18-19)

16. Explain whether it is better to choose between the three major theories or to use them all. (p. 19-20)

17. Describe 3 professional activities of social psychologists. (p. 20-21)

KEY TERMS

B=f(P,E)
behaviorism
cognition
cognitive structure
construct
distributive justice
field theory
gender-role norm
Gestalt psychology
hypothesis
interrole conflict
intrarole conflict
learning theory
norm
phenomenological approach
psychoanalytic theory
reinforcement
response
role
role expectations
role theory
schema
self-monitoring
social exchange theory
social facilitation
social learning theory
social psychology
socialization
S-R
S-O-R
stimulus
stimulus discrimination
stimulus generalization
superego
theory

COMPLETION ITEMS

Gordon Allport's classic definition of (1)____________ ______________ defines it as the field of study that attempts to understand how the thought, feeling, and (2)_______________ of individuals is influenced by the actual, imagined, or implied presence of other (3)_______________. Thus, things that people do alone (4)_______________ often of interest to social psychology.

Two major psychological theories dominated social psychology in the early 1900's. Watson's theory of (5)_____________ stressed the importance of learning and external stimuli. Freud's (6)________________ theory focused on (7)_______________causes of behavior. Gradually, modern social psychology emerged with an emphasis on both theory development and (8)________________ work.

One of the most influential early social psychologists was Kurt (9)____________. His (10)____________ theory stressed that B=f(P,E). This theory means that behavior is influenced by both the (11)_______________ and the (12)________________.

A logically consistent framework to integrate knowledge is called a (13)_________________. Specific terms or definitions called (14)____________________ serve to clarify concepts important to a theory. Theories not only summarize existing knowledge, they guide the development of predictions or (15)__________________. The process of testing (16)____________________ allows for the refinement of the (17)________________.

Three theories dominate current social psychology. (18)_______________ theory focuses on how an individual's behavior is influenced by the particular position(s) he or she occupies. A person's position such as student is called a (19)_______________. The role a person occupies results in certain assumptions about his or her behavior. These assumptions are called (20)______________ _______________. More generalized expectations which apply to just about anyone's behavior are called (21)________________. Sometimes a person is faced with incompatible expectations; these are called (22)_____________ ______________. When a person holds several positions (such as student and employee) which create incompatible demands, he or she is experiencing (23)______________ ______________. Conflict from incompatible expectations from within a single role (studying for a test or completing a term paper) illustrates (24)______________ ______________.

(25)______________ theory emphasizes the importance of the principles of reinforcement and learning. This theory looks at behavior in terms of S-R units. A (26)________________ is an external or internal event that serves as an occasion for a certain behavior or (27) _______________. If the behavior leads to a favorable outcome or (28)______________, the behavior is likely to be repeated. When a behavior starts occurring in settings similar to where it was reinforced, (29)_______________ ______________ has occurred. Learning to distinguish between stimulus conditions when behavior will and will not be reinforced involves (30)______________ ______________. According to (31)______________ ______________ theory a person may learn from observing another person's behavior and its consequences. (32)______________ ______________ theory is a learning theory which stresses that we seek out interactions with others which promise more rewards than costs.

Our thoughts (mental representations), and thought processes are emphasized in (33)______________ theory. Our mental representations are organized in ways that are useful to us. A bit of knowledge or a though is sometimes called a (34)______________. The organization of these thoughts is called cognitive (35)______________. Our thoughts and thought processes that deal with people represent (36)______________ ______________. One of the most widely used concepts referring to cognitive structure is (37)________________ which is an organization of knowledge based on past experience that we use to interpret our current experiences.

COMPLETION ITEM ANSWER KEY

(Answers printed in **bold type** require an exact match, but synonyms are acceptable for other items.)

1. **social psychology**
2. behavior
3. people
4. are
5. **behaviorism**
6. **psychoanalytic**
7. internal
8. experimental
9. **Lewin**
10. **field**
11. **person**
12. **environment**
13. **theory**
14. **constructs**
15. **hypotheses**
16. **hypothesis**
17. **theory**
18. **role**
19. **role**
20. **role expectations**
21. **norms**
22. **role conflicts**
23. **interrole conflict**
24. **intrarole conflict**
25. **learning**
26. **stimulus**
27. **response**
28. **reinforcement**
29. **stimulus generalization**
30. **stimulus discrimination**
31. **social learning**
32. **social exchange**
33. **cognitive**
34. **cognition**
35. **structure**
36. **social cognition**
37. **schema**

MULTIPLE CHOICE ITEMS

1. Which of the following is <u>not</u> within the realm of social psychology?
   a. the home court advantage in sports
   b. someone who falls down the stairs and develops a fear of heights
   c. a child who wants to grow up and be like mommy
   d. a student who copies his roommates term paper and worries about being caught

2. The field of social psychology developed:
   a. in ancient Greece about 800 B.C.
   b. during the 1600's
   c. during the late 1800's and early 1900's
   d. during the 1970's and 1980's

3. A ________ is a set of propositions created to organize the knowledge about a particular topic:
   a. theory
   b. construct
   c. hypothesis
   d. norm

4. Kurt Lewin's field theory suggests that a person's behavior is greatly influenced by:
   a. personal characteristics such as heredity, abilities, and state of health
   b. the social situation experienced by the person
   c. both (a) and (b)
   d. none of the above

5. In our society, people are expected to wear clothes in public. This expectation is an example of a:
   a. role expectation
   b. norm
   c. construct
   d. field theory

6. When Susan's mother is angry she frequently blurts out a string of four letter words. On her first day of kindergarten, Susan spilled her crayons and shouted a curse word. Which of the following theories best explains Susan's language:
   a. role theory
   b. cognitive theory
   c. social exchange theory
   d. social learning theory

7. According to Allport's definition, social psychology is an attempt to understand how the thought, feeling, and behavior of individuals are influenced by:
   a. the actual presence of others
   b. objective stimuli in the environment
   c. the imagined or implied presence of others
   d. both (a) and (c)

8. The first textbooks in social psychology were published in:
   a. 1612
   b. 1879
   c. 1908
   d. 1924

9. The major contribution of behaviorism to the development of social psychology was its focus on:
   a. internal mental events
   b. experimental methods
   c. environmental influences on behavior
   d. both (b) and (c)

10. Kurt Lewin's field theory saw behavior as influenced by both:
   a. the id and the ego
   b. the person and the environment
   c. needs and drives
   d. heredity and human nature

11. A theory is useful for:
   a. indicating gaps in knowledge
   b. guiding research
   c. organizing knowledge
   d. all of the above

12. Which of the following is <u>not</u> necessarily a characteristic of a good theory?
    a. logical consistency
    b. agreement with known facts
    c. testability
    d. complexity

13. Role theorists focus on how behavior is related to:
    a. the individual's position within a particular social context
    b. personality structures such as id, ego, and superego
    c. rewards and costs associated with the enactment of the behavior
    d. motivations

14. On the one hand, bus drivers should drive safely and courteously, should stop gently so passengers aren't jostled, and should wait their turn to merge with traffic. On the other hand, they should always remain on schedule, even if to do so involves driving aggressively. This illustrates:
    a. a poorly defined ego
    b. interrole conflict
    c. intrarole conflict
    d. what Freud called a "neurotogenic" role

15. Lieberman's (1965) study of the attitudes of factory workers demonstrated that:
    a. workers maintain remarkably consistent attitudes regardless of their relative position in the factory hierarchy
    b. position in the factory hierarchy seems to have considerable influence on worker attitudes
    c. unionization eliminates the attitudinal effect that might otherwise be produced by factory work
    d. management workers tend to be less flexible in their attitudes than are those in non-supervisory jobs

16. An internal or external event that brings about an alteration in a person's behavior is a:
    a. response
    b. stimulus
    c. defense mechanism
    d. trait

17. When Aron contributes to the class discussion, the professor praises him. As a result Aron increases his participation. Because it increased Aron's behavior, the professor's praise was a:
    a. stimulus
    b. generalization
    c. reinforcement
    d. role

18. A child had learned that sharing her toys with her sister at home results in approval from her parents. When she goes to school the first day, she offers her toy to another child during recess. This illustrates:
    a. stimulus generalization
    b. stimulus discrimination
    c. secondary reinforcement
    d. observational learning

19. In their theory of social learning, Bandura and his associates have placed special emphasis on:
    a. practice
    b. reinforcement
    c. motivation
    d. observation

20. Kelly and her roommate Laurie split the rent. Kelly does almost all the cleaning and buys more than half the food. However, Laurie has her boyfriend over all the time and they continually mess up the apartment. Kelly thinks her relationship with Laurie is unfair due to a lack of:
    a. self-monitoring
    b. social learning
    c. distributive justice
    d. role conflict

21. In Thibaut and Kelley's model, an outcome matrix is used to represent:
    a. the possible outcomes of an interaction
    b. all the outcomes a person has experienced in his or her previous relationships with others
    c. the process by which an individual determines what outcomes are rewarding
    d. all of the above

22. The representation of events in an individual's consciousness are stressed by:
    a. role theorists
    b. cognitive theorists
    c. behaviorists
    d. social learning theorists

23. Computer analogies of attitude structures are most likely to be used by:
    a. behaviorists
    b. psychoanalysts
    c. cognitive theorists
    d. psychometricians

24. How is the cognitive theorist most likely to analyze an interpersonal relationship? In terms of:
    a. rewards and costs
    b. childhood experiences
    c. the conflicts among various expectations and demands created by the roles involved in the relationship
    d. the individual's interpretations of each other's behavior

25. Which theory has the <u>least</u> historical emphasis?
    a. role theory
    b. reinforcement theory
    c. cognitive theory
    d. none of the above; they are all about the same

26. Which theory places the most emphasis on internal processes?
    a. role theory
    b. reinforcement theory
    c. cognitive theory
    d. behaviorism

27. Which theory places the <u>least</u> emphasis on individual differences?
    a. role theory
    b. reinforcement theory
    c. cognitive theory
    d. psychoanalysis

MULTIPLE CHOICE ANSWER KEY

1. b	6. d	11. d	16. b	21. a	26. c
2. c	7. d	12. d	17. c	22. b	27. a
3. a	8. c	13. a	18. a	23. c	
4. c	9. d	14. c	19. d	24. d	
5. b	10. b	15. b	20. c	25. a	

SHORT ANSWER ITEMS

1. What functions does a theory serve?

2. What are the characteristics of a good theory?

3. How do interrole and intrarole conflict differ? Give an example of each.

4. Describe the basic propositions of social exchange theory?

5. Describe the basic approach of cognitive theory.

6. Describe how role theory, learning theory, and cognitive theory explain social behavior.

APPLICATION QUESTIONS

Use relevant concepts from role theory, learning theory, and cognitive theory to develop three explanations for each of the patterns of behavior described in each of the examples listed below.

1. Susan is a secretary for a large insurance company. Several of the insurance agents are rude to her. She is upset by their behavior, but doesn't complain.

2. Allen is a junior in college and is vice president of his college fraternity. He is very bright, but spends little time studying and barely squeaks by. He spends most of his days and nights at the fraternity house talking, goofing off, or partying.

3. Kim and Steve have been dating for a couple of months. He wants to settle into a steady relationship, but she isn't sure. Several guys keep calling Kim to go out. She is tempted to go, but knows that Steve would be very upset. Finally, Kim decides to drop Steve.

CHAPTER TWO

METHODS OF STUDYING SOCIAL BEHAVIOR

CHAPTER OUTLINE

Research Hypotheses

- Testing Hypotheses

Major Methods of Social-Psychological Research

- Experimental Research
- Quasi-Experimental Research
- Field Research
- Archival Research
- Simulation Research
- Survey Research
- Selecting a Research Method

Simple Statistics

Ethics of Research

CHAPTER REVIEW

Conducting scientific research involves a series of steps. Hypotheses are testable predictions about behavior. Research involves developing hypotheses and getting information which allows the researcher to test hypotheses, and therefore, develop a more complete understanding of behavior. Hypotheses are generated in a variety of ways. Sometimes, they are carefully derived from theories. On other occasions, they are derived from previous research. At other times, hypotheses are distilled from informal observations of everyday experiences.

Hypotheses generally predict that certain conditions produce specified behavior. For example, one might hypothesize that aggression (a type of behavior) is more likely to occur following a frustrating experience (a condition). A condition thought to affect behavior is called an independent variable. The behavior is called the dependent variable because it is thought to depend on the independent variable. Thus, in the previous example, frustration is the independent variable and aggression is the dependent variable. Care is require to develop measures which accurately and consistently represent the theoretical variables that are of interest (such as frustration and aggression). It is also important to collect information in such a way that demand characteristics, evaluation apprehension, and experimenter expectancies do not influence subjects' behavior and result in findings that are not valid.

A variety of methods are available to collect information necessary to test a hypothesis. Each method has various strengths and weaknesses, so it is desirable to test a hypothesis with a variety of methods. Social psychology uses six different research methods: experiments, quasi-experimental research, field research, archival research, simulation, and survey research.

In an experiment, the researcher randomly assigns subjects to experimental conditions, manipulates one or more independent variables, and measures one or more dependent variables. Experiments allow randomization and careful control of independent variables, allowing for conclusions about cause and effect. But experiments have a number of potential problems such as a lack realism, demand characteristics, and evaluation apprehension. Quasi-experimental research examines subjects' behavior under different conditions, however, the experimenter does not have full experimental control over the independent variable.

Field research involves careful observation of behavior in natural settings. Archival research consists of examining existing records. Simulation research requires subjects to act as if they were in a particular situation, such as a conflict with another person or an inmate in a prison. Survey research involves collection of data by asking subjects to answer a series of questions, either through interviews or questionnaires. The accuracy of survey research depends on the accuracy of self-reports.

Ethical research does not harm the participants. Informed consent insures that subjects are aware of any potential hazards or stresses. If deception is necessary, a thorough debriefing in needed to explain the actual purpose of the study and the reason for the deception. The vast majority of social psychological research receives an ethical screening to insure that subjects are not subjected to risks.

LEARNING OBJECTIVES

After completing Chapter 2, you should be able to:

1. Describe a number of ways in which hypotheses can be formed. (p. 27)

2. Distinguish between the reliability and validity of a variable and explain the importance of each. (p. 28-29)

3. Explain and distinguish between independent and dependent variables. (p. 29)

4. Describe the importance of randomization and control in an experiment. (p. 31-33)

5. Describe the major advantages and disadvantages of an experiment. (p. 33-34)

6. Distinguish between experimental and quasi-experimental research. (p. 31-36)

7. Describe what is meant by field research, and summarize the major advantages and disadvantages of this technique. (p. 36-38)

8. Describe archival research and summarize its major advantages and disadvantages. (p. 38-40)

9. Discuss the advantages and disadvantages of simulation research. (p. 40-42)

10. Describe two major approaches to survey research. (p. 42-44).

11. Explain how survey research depends on the accuracy of self-report data and appropriate sampling. (p. 44)

12. Explain what types of information can be conveyed by measures of: central tendency, variability, and correlation. (p. 45-47)

13. Distinguish between main effects and interactions. (p. 47)

14. Describe the major ethical issues facing a person conducting social psychological research. (p. 47-49)

KEY TERMS

aggression
archival research
central tendency
correlation
debriefing
demand characteristics
dependent variable
evaluation apprehension
experiment
experimental realism
experimenter expectancies
external validity
field research
frustration
hypothesis
independent variable
informed consent
interaction
internal validity
interview
main effect
manipulation check
mean
meta-analysis
mundane realism
participant observer
quasi-experimental research
questionnaire
randomization
reliability
sampling procedures
self-report data
simulation
survey research
unobtrusive measure
validity
variability

COMPLETION ITEMS

Research involves testing predictions about behavior; these predictions are called (1)______________. Hypotheses usually indicate how behavior is affected by certain events or conditions. The measure of the research subject's behavior is called the (2)______________ ______________. The set of conditions that are hypothesized to affect dependent variable are called the (3)______________ ______________. Variables should be measured in ways that provide for consistent measurement or (4)______________. Proper measurement of variables requires that the measures actually reflect the intended concepts, thereby demonstrating (5)______________. The validity of a measure may be reduced by various procedural problems. Cues that indicate how subjects should act are called (6)______________ ______________ and reduce validity. Validity may also be reduced because of (7)______________ ______________, which occurs when participants are concerned about how others evaluate their behavior. Likewise, experimenters can inadvertently provide subtle indications of how they expect subjects to behave. These (8)______________ ______________ can reduce the validity of the dependent variable.

Various research methods are used to test (9)______________. In experiments, the researcher manipulates (10)______________ variables, and observes behavior to determine causal relationships. The researcher (11)______________ one or more independent variables, and observes one or more of the subject's behaviors. These behaviors are called (12)______________ variables. Through a process of (13)______________ subjects are assigned to different experimental conditions. These features of (14)______________ assignment to conditions, manipulation of (15)______________ variables and observation of (16)______________ variables allows the researcher to draw conclusions about (17)______________ and (18)______________ relationships.

An experiment that is highly involving for the subject is high in (19)______________ realism. An experimental situation that is similar to real world events is high in (20)______________ realism. Showing that the results of a laboratory experiment also apply to more natural settings serves to establish the (21)______________ ______________ of the laboratory findings. An experiment has high (22)______________ ______________ if the results were caused by the manipulations of the independent variables rather than by problems such as demand characteristics or evaluation apprehension.

A procedure in which the researcher cannot manipulate the independent variable, but can observe the behavior of persons who experience different conditions (such as comparisons of persons of different religions) represents (23)______________-______________ research. Because the researcher has less control than in an experiment, results must be interpreted (24)______________ cautiously.

A technique in which the researcher does not manipulate independent variables, but rather observes behavior in a natural setting represents (25)______________ ______________. When a researcher actively engages in the activities of a group in order to observe the behavior of the members, the researcher is acting as a (26)______________ ______________. Field research has the advantage of realism, but because it lacks the control of an experiment, it is difficult to make firm conclusions about (27)______________ and (28)______________.

A researcher who uses existing records such as crime rates or divorce records to test hypotheses is conducting (29)______________ ______________. Although archival research has many advantages, it is not always possible to find existing records that contain the information that is desired. Findings from a number of studies can be combined statistically to test hypotheses using a (30)______________-______________.

A study in which subjects take the role of the leader of a country and engage in mock negotiations is an example of (31)______________ research. In an (32)______________ the researcher talks with the subjects and asks questions. A (33)______________ consists of written questions that are answered by the subjects. Both interviews and questionnaires are examples of (34)______________ ______________. In order for the results of survey research to accurately represent the views or behavior of a specific population (such as North American college students), proper (35)______________ procedures must be used. At times, the results of survey research techniques are questioned because the data are based on (36)______________-______________

which may or may not be accurate. Since all research methods have weaknesses, greater understanding can be gained by testing the same hypothesis with a (37)______________ of methods.

Once data has been collected, researchers use a variety of statistics to interpret the results. Measures of (38)______________ ______________ provide a single number to reflect the average scores of a group of persons. Often researchers examine differences between the behavior of subjects who were or were not exposed to an independent variable. Experiments with more than one (39)______________ ______________ can reveal both main effects and interactions. An effect produced by one independent variable (such as the effect of status on aggression) is called a (40)______________ ______________. Sometimes the effect of one independent variable depends on the level or state of another independent variable. The statistical term for this is an (41)______________. Some research is concerned with how the level of one variable is associated with the level of another variable. For example, one study measured the association between amount of education and marital satisfaction. A (42)______________ measures such associations.

Research involves a variety of ethical concerns. The principle of (43)______________ ______________ involves telling subjects about the requirements of the experiment and obtaining their agreement to participate. However, sometimes researchers find it necessary to deceive subjects. In such instances, it is important that the experimenter conduct a thorough (44)______________ following the study. It is also important to maintain the (45)______________ of data so that unauthorized persons cannot learn about a subject's behavior or attitudes.

COMPLETION ITEM ANSWER KEY

(answers printed in **bold type** require an exact match, but synonyms are acceptable for other items.)

1. **hypotheses**
2. **dependent variable**
3. **independent variable**
4. **reliability**

23. **quasi-experimental**
24. more
25. **field research**
26. **participant observer**

5. **validity**
6. **demand characteristics**
7. **evaluation apprehension**
8. **experimenter expectancies**
9. **hypotheses**
10. **independent**
11. manipulates
12. **dependent**
13. **randomization**
14. **random**
15. **independent**
16. **dependent**
17. **cause**
18. **effect**
19. **experimental**
20. **mundane**
21. **external validity**
22. **internal validity**
27. cause
28. effect
29. **archival research**
30. **meta-analysis**
31. **simulation**
32. **interview**
33. **questionnaire**
34. **survey research**
35. **sampling**
36. **self-reports**
37. combination
38. **central tendency**
39. **independent variable**
40. **main effect**
41. **interaction**
42. **correlation**
43. **informed consent**
44. **debriefing**
45. confidentiality

MULTIPLE CHOICE ITEMS

1. The experimenter assigns subjects to 2 experimental conditions. Subjects in group 1 watch a movie of a bloody boxing match and subjects in group 2 watch a movie of a track meet. In what the subjects think is an unrelated study of learning, they deliver electrical shocks to another person when that person makes a mistake. The experimenter observes the severity of the shocks to see if the subjects in group 1 give more severe shocks than subjects in group 2. In this study, the amount of violence in the movie is:
   a. the independent variable
   b. the dependent variable
   c. a manipulation check
   d. the hypothesis

2. In the study described in question 1, the amount of shock given by the subjects is the:
   a. the independent variable
   b. the dependent variable
   c. a manipulation check
   d. the hypothesis

3. The experimenter in the study described in question 1 asked subjects to complete a questionnaire to verify that they thought the boxing match was more violent than the track meet. The questionnaire represents:
   a. the independent variable
   b. the hypothesis
   c. a manipulation check
   d. an unobtrusive measure

4. The experimenter who conducted the research described in question 1, thought that subjects who observed violence would give more severe shocks. This belief represents:
   a. the independent variable
   b. the dependent variable
   c. a manipulation check
   d. the hypothesis

5. Which of the following is a potential problem in a laboratory experiment?
   a. demand characteristics
   b. the artificiality of the setting
   c. experimenter expectancies
   d. all of the above

6. A researcher observes traffic at several locations to determine the number of people speeding, both before and after the state institutes a safe-driving campaign. This research is:
   a. an experiment
   b. archival research
   c. quasi-experimental research
   d. a simulation

7. A radio station in a large city urges its listeners to call in and tell who they prefer in the upcoming mayoral election. The listeners select candidate A, but candidate B is actually elected. This discrepancy is probably the result of:
   a. using survey research
   b. poor sampling procedures
   c. demand characteristics
   d. lack of mundane realism

8. The extent to which findings of research studies really apply to behavior in natural settings represents:
   a. experimental realism
   b. reliability of measurement
   c. internal validity
   d. external validity

9. A procedure for statistically combining the results of several studies to provide tests of hypotheses is a(n):
   a. meta-analysis
   b. survey technique
   c. correlation
   d. interaction

10. Based on the observation that TV commercials frequently show a celebrity praising a product, a researcher hypothesizes that a high-status communicator produces more attitude change than a low-status communicator. This is an example of hypothesis generation based on:
    a. trying to account for conflicting results
    b. accounting for paradoxical incident
    c. analyzing the practitioner's rule of thumb
    d. the hypothetico-deductive approach

11. Unobtrusive measures are useful because they:
    a. lead to more effective questionnaires
    b. do not require the use of statistics
    c. are required for a meta-analysis
    d. minimize problems of evaluation apprehension and demand characteristics

12. In an experiment, the researcher ______________ the independent variable and ______________ the dependent variable.
    a. measures, manipulates
    b. manipulates, measures
    c. holds constant, varies
    d. measures, holds constant

13. The procedure of randomly assigning subjects to conditions in an experiment:
    a. tends to ensure the similarity of subject characteristics across conditions
    b. ensures that results are relevant to natural settings
    c. makes the hypothesis more likely to be supported
    d. eliminates expectancy effects

14. As an experimental subject, you suspect that the experimenter wants you to agree with a message you have just been given to read. You do so, not because you really do agree, but in order to please the experimenter. In this case, your response may be said to be based on:
    a. external validity
    b. internal validity
    c. the dependent variable
    d. demand characteristics

15. Field research differs from an experiment in that the researcher:
    a. does not manipulate an independent variable
    b. does not make observations
    c. relies on data collected by other people, for other purposes than the research project
    d. all of the above

16. Examination of traffic court records in order to determine whether states that have harsh drunk driving laws have fewer alcohol-related traffic violations than states with weak laws would be an example of:
    a. archival research
    b. a field study
    c. participant observation
    d. a field experiment

17. The Zimbardo prison study discussed in the text demonstrates that in simulation research:
    a. it is difficult to get subjects to take the situation seriously
    b. ethical issues seldom arise
    c. subjects can become very involved in a simulation
    d. random assignment of subjects is almost impossible

18. The use of role play and simulation techniques is controversial because:
    a. subjects are not provided with an opportunity to give informed consent
    b. subjects may respond only as they <u>think</u> they would act in a real situation, not as they <u>actually</u> would behave
    c. it is very hard to get subjects to agree to participate in such studies
    d. their results cannot be replicated

19. Calvin is a subject in an experiment and knows his behavior is being observed. He changes his normal behavior so that he can create a more favorable impression. His behavior reflects:
    a. experimenter expectancies
    b. a manipulation check
    c. evaluation apprehension
    d. external validity

20. The average response of a group of people is a measure of:
    a. reliability
    b. association
    c. variability
    d. central tendency

21. Variability refers to:
    a. the dispersion of responses
    b. the average response of a group of people
    c. how closely two variables are related to one another
    d. the difference between two groups

22. You conducted an experiment in which a male or female subject was praised by either a male or female experimenter. You measured the subject's subsequent liking for the experimenter. What was the dependent variable in your study?
    a. praise
    b. sex of the experimenter
    c. sex of the subject
    d. subject's liking for the experimenter

23. In the above study, if you had found that the only difference between your groups was that female experimenters were liked best by all subjects, what kind of effect would you have?
    a. a main effect
    b. an interaction
    c. a correlation effect
    d. a meta-effect

24. When the effect of one independent variable depends on the level of another independent variable, we have a(n):
    a. main effect
    b. interaction
    c. correlation
    d. probable error

25. During the debriefing, the experimenter:
    a. manipulates the independent variable
    b. reveals the complete procedure to the subject
    c. usually has to deceive the subject
    d. measures the dependent variable

26. A questionnaire designed to measure leadership ability yields identical scores each time it is given to a subject. This consistency demonstrates the ______________ of the question.
    a. reliability
    b. validity
    c. experimental realism
    d. mundane realism

27. If a person's score on a leadership questionnaire has nothing to do with his or her ability to lead, the questionnaire lacks ______________.
    a. reliability
    b. validity
    c. experimental realism
    d. mundane realism

28. Which research technique is best?
    a. an experiment
    b. field research
    c. survey research
    d. no technique is best, all have strengths and weaknesses

MULTIPLE CHOICE ANSWER KEY

1. a	6. c	11. d	16. a	21. a	26. a
2. b	7. b	12. b	17. c	22. d	27. b
3. c	8. d	13. a	18. b	23. a	28. d
4. d	9. a	14. d	19. c	24. b	
5. d	10. c	15. a	20. d	25. b	

SHORT ANSWER ITEMS

1. List five sources of hypotheses.

2. Describe the basic logic of an experiment. Distinguish between independent and dependent variables.

3. Describe the ethical problems involved in social psychological research.

4. Describe the major advantages and disadvantages of the six research methods discussed in this chapter: experimental research, quasi-experimental research, field research, archival research, simulation research, and survey research.

CHAPTER THREE

THE SELF

CHAPTER OUTLINE

The Nature of the Self

- Theories of the Development of Self
- The Structure of the Self-Concept
- Influences on Self-Development

Becoming Aware of the Self

- A Theory of Self-Perception
- States of Self-Awareness
- Individual Differences in Self-Awareness

Dealing with the Self

- Self-Esteem
- Experiencing Emotions
- Exploring the Self

Relating to Others

- Presenting the Self
- The Goals of Self-Presentation
- Self-Handicapping and BIRGing
- Individual Differences in Self-Presentation

CHAPTER REVIEW

Our self-concept consists of all the thoughts and feelings we have about ourselves. Interactions with other people greatly influence a person's self-concept. Terms such as "looking-glass self" and "reflected appraisals" emphasize that the reactions of others affect a person's self-concept. A person's self-concept is also influenced by reflections on his or her actions and the effects of those actions. The specific parts of our self-concept that we are most aware vary across situations. That is, you may think about your appearance or popularity when among friends, but think about other aspects of yourself when with your parents.

We are not always actively aware of ourselves, but at times, we focus our attention on some facet of ourself, and experience self-awareness. People differ in their tendencies to think about the self, called self-consciousness. Private self-consciousness involves focusing on internal aspects of the self, such as beliefs, moods, and bodily sensations. Public self-consciousness relates to concerns about how others view us and what they think of us.

Self-esteem refers to our positive or negative evaluation of ourself. Comparisons between how we see ourself and how we think we should be or would like to be can produce emotions. Large discrepancies produce negative emotions such as guilt, or disappointment. Close correspondence between our behavior and our standards may produce positive emotions such as satisfaction and happiness.

We often engage in a process of social comparison in order to evaluate our values, skills, or abilities by comparing ourself to others. On some occasions, we do not seek an accurate assessment of ourself, but want to bolster our view of ourself (self-enhancement). Self-enhancement often involves the use of a self-serving attribution bias. This bias occurs when we take full credit for our successes, but explain away our failures.

Because people are concerned with how others see them, they engage in impression management. We use a variety of self- presentation strategies to help create the desired impressions. Persons high in self-monitoring are skilled at learning what behavior is socially appropriate and can control their behavior to create the desired impressions. Self-presentation strategies are not necessarily used to be deceptive, we may merely use them to convey an honest impression.

LEARNING OBJECTIVES

After Completing Chapter 3, you should be able to:

1. Explain why the self is an important part of social psychology. (p. 52-53)

2. Explain what is meant by a self-schema, how self-schemas are formed and how they influence our thoughts and behavior. (p. 53-55)

3. Explain how the self-concept can be relatively stable, but still vary across situations. (p. 55-56)

4. Describe the basic factors which determine the nature of a person's self-concept. (p. 56-60)

5. Describe the factors that activate self-awareness, and the major effects of self-awareness. (p. 60-66)

6. Distinguish between self-consciousness and self-awareness. (p. 60-63)

7. Describe and distinguish between private and public self-consciousness. (p. 63 and 76)

8. Distinguish between self-concept and self-esteem. (p. 53-58 and 63-65)

9. Describe the ways in which self-awareness may lead to negative emotions. (p. 65-66)

10. Describe three reasons for social comparison. (p. 67)

11. For each of the three reasons for social comparison, describe the nature of persons that are chosen for comparison. (p. 67-68)

12. Explain the self-serving attribution bias. (p. 68-69)

13. Discuss the ethics of impression management. (p. 70-71)

14. Describe five self-presentation strategies. (p. 71-73)

15. Explain self-handicapping and explain its causes and consequences. (p. 73-74)

16. Use the Self-Evaluation Maintenance Model to explain why we can use such a variety of self-presentation strategies. (p. 75)

17. Describe the differences in behavior of persons high and low in self-monitoring. (76-78)

KEY TERMS

bask in reflected glory
causal attribution
confirmatory bias
exemplification
gender identity
ideal self
impression management
ingratiation
intimidation
ought self
priming
private self-consciousness
public self-consciousness
racial identity
reflected appraisal
schema
self-affirmation
self-awareness
self-concept
self-consciousness
self-enhancement
self-esteem
self-handicapping strategy
self-monitoring
self-perception theory
self-presentation
self-promotion
self-schema
self-serving attribution bias
social comparison theory
supplication
working self-concept

COMPLETION ITEMS

All the thoughts that a person has about himself or herself make up the person's (1)______________-______________. The term looking-glass self emphasizes that a person's self-concept reflects the evaluations of others. A related term, (2)______________ appraisal was also used to describe this process by which our impressions of ourself are based on the impressions of (3)______________.

The cognitive concept of schema has been applied to thoughts about oneself; cognitive generalizations, or organizations of thought about oneself are called

(4)_______________-_______________. Self-schemas reflect the ways we think about (5)_______________. The contents of self-schemas vary somewhat from person to person. Because our gender is so obvious, (6)_______________ _______________ is often an important part of one's self-concept. Likewise, a person's self-concept often includes an awareness of his or her race, called a (7)_______________ _______________. We are not always aware of all facets of the self-concept. The aspects of a person's self-concept which are currently on their mind are called the (8)_______________ _______________-_______________.

The suggestion that we observe and think about our own behavior and draw inferences about the self is emphasized in (9)_______________-_______________ _______________. At certain times, such as when a person glances at a mirror, he or she may focus attention on some facet of the self. This self-reflection has been termed (10)_______________-_______________. Some people are more likely than others to engage in self-reflection. The degree to which a person engages in self-reflection illustrates their level of (11)_______________-_______________. Reflecting on personal aspects of the self such as moods and feelings involves (12)_______________ _______________-_______________. Concern with how others see you or what they think of you reflects (13)_______________ _______________-_______________.

The extent to which we feel positively or negatively about ourself reflects our (14)_______________-_______________. We often compare our self with some standards we set for ourselves. An image of what we would like to be is an (15)_______________ self. Our (16)_______________ _______________ represents what we feel we should be. When we don't live up to these standards we may experience negative (17)_______________. Often, we evaluate our beliefs, skills, or behavior by comparing ourself with others.
This process illustrates Festinger's (18)_______________ _______________ theory. Sometimes the goal of social comparison is to gain information for accurate self-evaluation or to help us improve our performance. At other times, social comparison is used as an attempt to convince us that we are better than we really are. This goal is called (19)_______________-_______________.

People interpret the reasons why people (including themselves) act in particular ways. The process of inferring causes of behavior is termed (20)______________ ______________. Behavior can be attributed to qualities of the person or to the environment. The tendency to accept greater responsibility for our own positive outcomes than for our negative outcomes reflects a (21)______________-______________ ______________ ______________.

The process of (22)______________ ______________ describes our attempts to create certain images or impressions. Behavior such as agreeing with another or giving compliments simply to be liked are examples of (23)______________. Trying to control others by causing them to fear us illustrates (24)______________. Trying to impress others by describing our accomplishments or abilities involves (25)______________-______________. Trying to make others feel guilty because we work so hard or give up so much for them is an example of (26)______________. A person who says he or she can't type or change a tire in hopes that another will do it is using (27)______________. (28)______________- ______________ is the technique of having a built-in excuse for failure. Wanting to associate with popular or famous people in order to impress others involves trying to (29)______________ in (30)______________ ______________. Persons high in (31)______________-______________ are skilled at reading other people and adjusting their behavior to fit the situation.

COMPLETION ITEM ANSWER KEY

(Answers printed in **bold type** require an exact match, but synonyms are acceptable for other items).

1. **self-concept**
2. **reflected**
3. others
4. **self-schema**
5. ourselves
6. **gender identity**
7. **racial identity**
8. **working self-concept**
9. **self-perception theory**
10. **self-awareness**
11. **self-consciousness**
12. **private self-consciousness**
16. **ought self**
17. emotions
18. **social comparison**
19. **self-enhancement**
20. **causal attribution**
21. **self-serving attribution bias**
22. **impression management**
23. **ingratiation**
24. **intimidation**
25. **self-promotion**
26. **exemplification**
27. **supplication**

13. **public self-consciousness**
14. **self-esteem**
15. **ideal**
28. **self-handicapping**
29. **bask**
30. **reflected glory**
31. **self-monitoring**

MULTIPLE CHOICE ITEMS

1. Our self-concept is influenced by:
   a. what other people think of us
   b. characteristics such as race and gender
   c. our self-perceptions
   d. all of the above

2. Which of the following statements is <u>false</u>:
   a. a person's self-concept has many facets
   b. the contents of the self-schema varies from person to person
   c. the self-concept is a purely personal experience and is not influenced by other people
   d. a self-schema may include visual images such as personal appearances

3. Diversity or complexity in a person's self-concept:
   a. is likely to cause an identity crisis
   b. may provide a buffer against stressful events
   c. makes self-monitoring difficult
   d. eliminates the need for social comparison

4. A person's self-concept is likely to include:
   a. thoughts about the person's gender
   b. features which set him or her apart from others
   c. things that are important to one's friends on the broader culture
   d. all of the above

5. The notion that we can gain an understanding of what we are like by paying attention to our behavior is the central notion of:
   a. social comparison theory
   b. self-perception theory
   c. self-schema theory
   d. self-monitoring theory

6. The notion that we judge ourselves by seeing how we stack up against others is derived from:
   a. social comparison theory
   b. self-perception theory
   c. self-schema theory
   d. self-monitoring theory

7. Awareness of our moods and feelings reflects:
   a. self-monitoring
   b. self-schema
   c. private self-consciousness
   d. social comparison

8. Self-awareness is most likely to occur when:
   a. a person is sleeping
   b. a person is being stared at by others
   c. a person is studying for an exam
   d. a person is absorbed in a book

9. A person sees several persons jogging and is reminded of his or her physical self. This is an example of:
   a. priming
   b. causal attribution
   c. self-monitoring
   d. self-presentation

10. Jake is very concerned with how others see him. He is high in:
   a. self-esteem
   b. private self-consciousness
   c. public self-consciousness
   d. ingratiation

11. Morgan wants to hit a home run, but can only hit singles. As a result he feels disappointed. This is caused by:
   a. a discrepancy between his actual self and his ideal self
   b. a discrepancy between his ought self and his ideal self
   c. a lack of objective self-awareness
   d. too little self-monitoring

12. Which of the following statements is <u>true</u>?
    a. People think about themselves more than anything else
    b. There is essentially no difference in the self-schemas different people have
    c. People who are high in private self-consciousness cannot deal with stress
    d. Thinking about the self is not necessarily a positive experience

13. Which of the following statements is <u>true</u>?
    a. Self-serving attribution bias is rare
    b. Self-serving attribution bias involves taking full responsibility for our failures
    c. Self-serving attribution bias is less common in chronically depressed persons than in others
    d. all of the above

14. Professor Smith wants students to fear him and study hard for his class. On the first day of class he comes off like "Rambo" and makes a very fierce impression. He is practicing the techniques of:
    a. objective self-awareness
    b. intimidation
    c. self-handicapping
    d. exemplification

15. During the first week of school Linda tells you that in high school she was class president and homecoming queen. She is hoping to impress you. Her behavior illustrates:
    a. self-promotion
    b. ingratiation
    c. intimidation
    d. supplication

16. Persons high in self-monitoring:
    a. are sensitive to the subtle expressions of others
    b. are good at learning what is socially appropriate in new settings
    c. are skilled at creating the impressions they want
    d. all of the above

17. A tall person would be most likely to mention height as an unstructured self-description when he or she is:
    a. from a large family
    b. taller than others in his or her environment
    c. the same height as most other people in the environment
    d. an only child

18. You see yourself as a very outgoing person, and you tend to organize other information about yourself around your sociability. In this case, your outgoing behavior serves as the basis of a:
    a. self-handicapping strategy
    b. self-schema
    c. social comparison
    d. cognitive label for arousal

19. Self-esteem refers to:
    a. the components of the self
    b. how we present ourselves to others
    c. evaluative (good/bad) judgments about the self
    d. fairly unstable assessments of self

20. If a person realizes that no matter how hard he or she tries that it is not possible to perform up to the desired standard, he or she is likely to:
    a. continue to seek opportunities for evaluation
    b. avoid self-awareness
    c. like self-evaluation
    d. bask in reflected glory

21. After an entire summer at tennis camp, Jim still can't make his high school tennis team. He concludes that "I'm not a very good tennis player." This is an example of a(n):
    a. self-serving attribution
    b. self-perception
    c. ingratiation
    d. intimidation

22. A self-serving attributional bias is seen when people seek:
    a. situational causes for failure and dispositional causes for success
    b. dispositional causes for failure and situational causes for success
    c. situational causes for all outcomes
    d. dispositional causes for all outcomes

23. When people engage in social comparison, the goal is:
    a. an accurate assessment of oneself
    b. information that can be used for self-improvement
    c. self-enhancement
    d. any of the above may be the goal of social comparison

24. The study of collegiate swimmers indicated that compared to those with low self-handicapping tendencies, those individuals with a high tendency toward self-handicapping tended to practice:
    a. more before important meets
    b. less before important meets
    c. more before unimportant meets
    d. less before unimportant meets

25. Self-handicapping strategies seem to be used to:
    a. convince others that we are not very capable
    b. bask in glory reflected by others
    c. developing accurate self-perceptions
    d. maintain a positive self-concept or the image of competence even if the person performs poorly

26. Complimenting your boss on her clothing in an attempt to gain her favor is an example of:
    a. supplication
    b. exemplification
    c. ingratiation
    d. self-promotion

27. William James's (1890) conception of the self:
    a. is very outdated now and not accepted by contemporary psychologists
    b. suggested that the self is unidimensional (having only one component)
    c. has continued to influence theorists
    d. portrayed the self as independent of social influences

28. When Ben catches lots of fish, he thinks it reflects his skill. When he can't get a bite, he blames it on the poor fishing conditions. This represents:
    a. social comparison
    b. private self-consciousness
    c. exemplification
    d. self-serving attribution bias

MULTIPLE CHOICE ANSWER KEY

1. d	6. a	11. a	16. d	21. b	26. c
2. c	7. c	12. d	17. b	22. a	27. c
3. b	8. b	13. c	18. b	23. d	28. d
4. d	9. a	14. b	19. c	24. b	
5. b	10. c	15. a	20. b	25. d	

SHORT ANSWER ITEMS

1. What does it mean to say that we have multiple identities or multiple self-schemas?

2. What determines the content of a person's self-concept?

3. Distinguish between self-awareness and self-consciousness.

4. Distinguish between private and public self-consciousness.

5. When does a person engage in social comparison? With whom does a person compare himself or herself? How is this affected by the goal of social comparison?

6. Is impression management deceptive and unethical?

APPLICATION QUESTIONS

1. Answer the following question: Who am I?

2. What factors have influenced the contents of your self-concept?

3. Describe a time when you engaged in social comparison. What was your goal or reason for social comparison?

4. Describe an example in which you or someone you know has used each of the following self-presentation strategies:

   A. ingratiation

B. intimidation

C. self-promotion

D. exemplification

E. supplication

F. self-handicapping

G. basking in reflected glory

CHAPTER FOUR

UNDERSTANDING OTHERS

CHAPTER OUTLINE

CHAPTER REVIEW

Our initial impressions of a person are often based on characteristics such as sex, race, and physical appearance. We often use such surface information to make inferences about a person's personality or character. Our judgments of another are often expressed in terms of that person's personality traits. Our overall impression of another person seems to be a composite or weighted average of the traits we judge the person to possess. Traits that are of greater importance to us have more influence in our overall impression.

Our patterns of thinking can influence our thoughts about a person. Philosophies of human nature describe our general conception of what people are like. Implicit personality theories are vague assumptions that some personality traits are usually associated with other traits. Cognitive structures, such as schemas, prototypes, stereotypes and scripts are used to organize our thinking about people and social events.

When we try to interpret why persons act as they do, we make causal attributions, judgments about the causes of behavior. We can explain the behavior as caused by the person engaging in the behavior (actor), the target of the behavior (entity), or the circumstances. Information about the consistency of the actor's behavior, how others act in the same situation (consensus), and the extent to which the behavior occurs in limited settings (distinctiveness) are useful guides to causal attribution. Our attributions are also based on the effects of the behavior and effects of possible alternative behaviors. Noncommon effects are outcomes that result from the chosen behavior, but which would not result from other possible alternative behaviors. When there is only one, or there are at most a few noncommon effects, it is easier to interpret the cause of the actor's behavior.

The information processing model of Fiske & Neuberg describes how our existing cognitive structures affect our impressions of a person. First, we form an initial categorization based on factors such as occupation, gender, or group membership. If we continue to think about the person, we often seek additional information to confirm our initial categorization. Our interpretation of ambiguous events may be biased to support our initial categorization. If the information clearly does not fit our existing categorization, we may modify the categorization or form a more individualized impression of the person by piecing together our judgments of the person's traits.

Our attempts to know other persons are not completely accurate. They are limited by a variety of biases such as: false consensus bias, the fundamental attribution error, and belief in a just world.

LEARNING OBJECTIVES

After completing chapter 4, you should be able to:

1. Explain why it is important to be able to understand and interpret the behavior of others. (p. 82)

2. Describe how we use physical appearance in forming impressions. (p. 82-84)

3. Describe two central dimensions that summarize many of the traits we use to describe other people. (p. 86)

4. Distinguish between global and circumscribed accuracy (p. 88).

5. Explain how implicit personality theories are used to expand what we think we know about another person. (p. 88-89)

6. Explain how cognitive structures such as schemas influence our knowledge of others. (p 92)

7. Describe the conditions which make it likely that an illusory correlation will be perceived. (p 96)

8. Describe how the stages of initial categorization, confirmation, recategorization, and information integration fit into an overall process of impression formation. (p. 96-101)

9. Explain the use of the weighted averaging model of information integration. (p. 100)

10. Define causal attribution. (p. 102)

11. Discuss how consensus, consistency, and distinctiveness are used in making causal attributions. (p. 103)

12. Explain the use of discounting and augmentation. (p. 104)

13. Define a noncommon effect. (p. 106)

14. Explain the importance of noncommon effects in making causal attributions. (p. 106)

15. Describe the fundamental attribution bias. (p. 107)

16. Describe Weiner's 3 basic dimensions and their use in explaining success and failure. (p. 109).

17. Explain how our explanation of a person's success or failure can affect our reaction to them. (110)

18. Explain how the belief in a just world may influence our attributions. (p. 111).

KEY TERMS

actor
actor observer effect
augmentation principle
availability heuristic
belief in a just world
category-based expectancies
causal attribution
causal schema
central trait
circumscribed accuracy
consensus
consistency
construct
controllability
discounting
dispositional attribution
distinctiveness
entity
false consensus bias
fundamental attribution bias
global accuracy
heuristic
illusory correlation
implicit personality theory
locus of causality
multiple necessary cause schema
multiple sufficient cause schema
noncommon effects
philosophies of human nature
priming
prototype
representativeness heuristic
schema
script
situational attribution
social theory
stability
stereotype
target-based expectancies
vividness
weighted averaging model

COMPLETION ITEMS

Our impressions of another person are influenced by surface characteristics such as sex, race, and physical appearance. With respect to physical attractiveness, we seem to act as if what is beautiful is (1)______________. Studies show that physical (2)______________ can influence judgments of many characteristics such as suitability for a job, psychological adjustment, or the quality of one's work. Traits that have great influence on our overall impression of another are called (3)______________ ______________. The centrality of a trait is greater when it provides new information. If we conclude that a person has a particular trait, and this trait allows us to correctly predict his or her behavior in a wide variety of situations, then our impression has (4)______________ accuracy. But if the trait only predicts the behavior in specific situations, it represents (5)______________ ______________. Traits vary in how positive or negative they are. Since some traits are more important to us, our overall impression can be best predicted by the (6)______________ ______________ model.

Each of us has general expectations about what people are like. These general assumptions of people are called (7)______________ _____ ______________ ______________. An unstated assumption that certain traits go together (i.e., intelligent people are friendly) is called an (8)______________ ______________ ______________. A general belief about how certain events are related (i.e., exercise improves moods) is called a (9)______________ ______________. An organization of knowledge that we develop based on past experience and use to interpret our current experiences is called a (10)______________. We have many (11)______________ about other people. The term (12)______________ describes a category of persons such as a rock star or a truck driver and the behaviors and characteristics thought to characterize such a person. A set of thoughts about a typical sequence of events is a (13)______________. Cognitive categorizations such as schemas, prototypes, and scripts influence how we interpret, remember, and evaluate social events. A schema about a particular category of people which, like a prototype, describes the expected behavior and characteristics of that category of people is called a (14)______________.

The particular schema used to categorize or organize thoughts may influence the interpretation and recall of information. Events that fit a preexisting (15)______________ are recalled more rapidly than those that don't.

The process of forming an impression can involve up to four steps. Initially pigeonholing a person into an existing category such as sorority girl, elderly, or athlete represents the (16)______________ ______________. We sometimes distort information to make it fit our initial categorization. This represents a (17)______________ bias. If we can't make the information fit our existing categorization (as when a husband is not employed and cares for the children and housework), we may create more specific subcategories (such as house husband). Revising our initial categories in this way is called (18)______________. If we cannot fit our knowledge into one of our existing categories or subcategories, we may carefully consider each of the person's traits and build up a unique impression of the person. This is referred to as (19)______________ ______________.

Making inferences concerning the reasons why a person acted in a particular way illustrates the process of (20)______________ ______________. Behavior may be caused by the person, illustrating a (21)______________ cause. Behavior may also be attributed to environmental or (22)______________ causes. When making attributions, we often look for patterns. If the person shows the same behavior on different occasions, this provides (23)______________ information. If many people show the same behavior, we have (24)______________ information. High (25)______________ indicates that the behavior occurs only under certain circumstances. Depending upon the pattern of consistency, consensus, and distinctiveness information, we can attribute the behavior to the actor, entity, or circumstances. Deciding that Susan slapped Mike because she is a hothead is making an attribution to the (26)______________. Inferring that Mike must have provoked Susan to bring on the slap is an example of an attribution to the (27)______________. Realizing that Susan only slapped Mike because they were practicing their parts in a play illustrates making an (28)______________ to the circumstances.

When making attributions, we not only look at the behavior, but also its effects or consequences. We also look at possible alternative behaviors and the (29)______________ of these actions. An effect which results from the chosen action, but would not result from the alternative behavior is a (30)______________ ______________. The (31)______________ the number of noncommon effects, the more likely we are to attribute the behavior to characteristics of the (32)______________.

The tendency to focus on the actor as the cause of the behavior and thus fail to fully consider environmental causes of the behavior is called (33)______________ ______________ ______________. Believing that people get what they deserve has been termed belief in a (34)______________ ______________.

Weiner's attribution model deals with explanations for (35)______________ and (36)______________. Based on his model, causes of behavior may be classified as internal or external and (37)______________ or (38)______________.

COMPLETION ITEM ANSWER KEY

(Answers printed in **bold type** require an exact match, but synonyms are acceptable for other items.)

1. good
2. attractiveness
3. **central traits**
4. **global**
5. **circumscribed accuracy**
6. **weighted averaging**
7. **assumptions about human nature**
8. **implicit personality theory**
9. **social theory**
10. **schema**
11. **schemas**
12. **prototype**
13. **script**
14. **stereotype**
15. **schema**
16. **initial categorization**
19. **information integration**
20. **causal attribution**
21. dispositional
22. situational
23. **consistency**
24. **consensus**
25. **distinctiveness**
26. actor
27. entity
28. **attribution**
29. effects
30. **noncommon effect**
31. fewer
32. actor
33. **fundamental attribution error**
34. **just world**
35. success

17. **confirmatory**
18. **recategorization**

36. failure
37. stable
38. temporary

MULTIPLE CHOICE ITEMS

1. If we meet an attractive person, our evaluation of the person is likely to be:
   a. negative because we are envious of their looks
   b. positive because we seem to think that good looks are associated with positive traits
   c. unaffected by the person's appearance
   d. high in global accuracy

2. Allen lives on your floor in the dorm. When you are around, he jokes around quite a bit. You infer that he is "happy-go-lucky". This interpretation accurately portrays his behavior in the dorm, but at work, or in class he is all business. Your impression of Allen shows:
   a. a complete lack of accuracy
   b. circumscribed accuracy
   c. global accuracy
   d. weighted accuracy

3. April's boss asks if she knows anyone who might want a job. The person must be friendly, intelligent, dependable, and honest. April thinks of Julie, the person who sits next to her in class. Based on classroom behavior April knows that Julie is friendly, intelligent, and dependable. April assumes that Julie must also be honest because she thinks that friendly, dependable, people must be honest. This illustrates:
   a. April's implicit personality theory
   b. April's philosophy of human nature
   c. Julie's prototype
   d. Julie's script

4. You decide to attend church services with a friend. You expect certain things to occur such as hymns, a sermon, and prayer. Such expectations reflect a:
   a. philosophy of human nature
   b. implicit personality theory
   c. prototype
   d. script

5. Adults whose facial features resemble those of infants:
   a. are considered attractive
   b. are assumed to be less dominant and less smart
   c. are more likely to use prototypes in their judgments of others
   d. are less likely to use prototypes in their judgments of others

6. Albert works with Janice who is a redhead. She is very silly so he tends to think that redheads are silly. This represents:
   a. a central trait
   b. circumscribed accuracy
   c. the use of the weighted averaging model
   d. an illusory correlation

7. According to the false consensus bias, a student who likes country music is likely to _____ the percentage of students who like country music.
   a. underestimate
   b. overestimate
   c. know
   d. not care about

8. Jim and Jane go out often. He is usually about 15 to 30 minutes late and is often late for other appointments. Jane is likely to attribute Jim's behavior to:
   a. the entity
   b. the circumstances
   c. a temporary internal dimension
   d. a stable internal dimension

9. Mr. Moore manages the branch office of a bank. One night, people broke into his house, held his family hostage and threatened to kill them if he didn't drive one of them to the bank and turn over all the money. Mr. Moore gaves them $20,000 of the bank's money to save his family. Which principle explains why Mr. Moore was not considered to be a thief even though he took the bank's money.
   a. belief in a just world
   b. a noncommon effect
   c. discounting
   d. the false consensus bias

10. A student asks a question in class and the professor gets very upset. The professor calls the student stupid and asks if the student knows how to read. You observe the incident and conclude that the professor must be hostile and that the student must have asked a stupid question. Your attribution may reflect a causal schema based on:
   a. discounting
   b. weighted averaging
   c. the multiple sufficient cause model
   d. the multiple necessary cause model

11. Anna has two job offers. She chooses to work in Hawaii as a travel agent making $100,000 per year for a nice boss rather than work cooking hamburgers for minimum wage in Kansas for an unpleasant boss. It would be hard to interpret the exact reason for her behavior because:
   a. there are several noncommon effects
   b. there are too few noncommon effects
   c. we do not know Anna's philosophy of human nature
   d. Anna is demonstrating her implicit personality theory

12. Carolyn is working hard to complete her term paper that is due the next day. Nancy asks if she wants to go to a movie, and Carolyn explains that she can't go. Nancy incorrectly concludes that Carolyn is unfriendly. This attribution may reflect:
   a. belief in a just world
   b. a script
   c. priming
   d. a fundamental attribution error

13. You learn that an old friend is engaged to a man from a small town who drives a pickup. You haven't met him, but think he must be a hick and figure she has picked a real looser. Your judgment represents:
    a. a causal attribution
    b. information integration
    c. initial categorization
    d. recategorization

14. When you find that the country man your friend wants to marry is a successful veterinarian, you decide that she made a good catch. Your change of opinion represents:
    a. a causal attribution
    b. information integration
    c. initial categorization
    d. recategorization

15. Catherine is a woman of average weight and usually blends in with the crowd. If she attends a meeting of "overeaters anonymous" she stands out because she is so much thinner than everyone else. She is noticed so much in this setting because of:
    a. vividness
    b. distinctiveness
    c. a central trait
    d. a schema

16. When consistency is high, consensus is low, and distinctiveness is low. The attribution will generally be made to:
    a. the actor
    b. the entity
    c. the circumstances
    d. the situation

17. Frank rarely laughs at movies, but watches a new movie and laughs from start to finish. The entire audience is also laughing. We are likely to explain Frank's behavior by an attribution to:
    a. Frank
    b. the movie
    c. a causal schema
    d. a category-based expectancy

18. Attempts to infer causes or explanations for observed behavior are called:
    a. stereotyping
    b. causal attribution
    c. schemas
    d. constructive biases

19. Central traits are those that:
    a. carry greater weight than others, influencing the overall impression
    b. stand out in our minds as being particularly characteristic of certain individuals
    c. are characteristic of the majority of people in a given population
    d. are evaluatively extreme

20. Anticipation of a similar fate results in:
    a. increased victim blaming
    b. decreased victim blaming
    c. more derogation of a victim
    d. ignoring injustice

21. According to Kelley's attribution model, attributions to the actor are made when:
    a. consensus is low, consistency is high, and distinctiveness is low
    b. consensus is high, consistency is high, and distinctiveness is high
    c. consistency is low
    d. consensus is high and consistency is low

22. According to research concerning correspondent inferences, attributions about an actor's personality are most likely when:
    a. a behavior is expected and noncommon effects are numerous
    b. a behavior is unexpected and noncommon effects are numerous
    c. a behavior is unexpected and noncommon effects are few
    d. a behavior is expected and noncommon effects are few

23. In Weiner's model, effort represents an attribution that is:
    a. external and stable
    b. external and temporary
    c. internal and temporary
    d. internal and stable

24. Attribution of successful performance to unstable cause is likely to result in:
    a. low expectations for future performance
    b. high expectations for future performance
    c. punishment
    d. reward

25. The fundamental attribution bias leads us to overemphasize:
    a. situational causes
    b. temporary causes
    c. dispositional causes
    d. external causes

26. Allison and Walter are college seniors with the same faculty advisor. This week, both went to see her. Allison caught her at a good time, and she was very helpful, but Walter dropped by when she was too busy to see him. Based on this recent experience, they give different answers when someone asks if college faculty are helpful. The large impact of a recent experience illustrates:
    a. the representativeness heuristic
    b. the just world hypothesis
    c. information integration
    d. weighted averaging

27. Cognitive structures such as schemas and prototypes affect:
    a. the processing of information about a person
    b. the recall of information about a person
    c. the way we react to people
    d. all of the above

28. Kelly returns home to find her apartment engulfed in a raging fire. At great risk, she rushes in and rescues her puppy that is trapped inside. We are likely to be especially confident that she cares deeply for her puppy because of:
    a. the false consensus bias
    b. consistency
    c. the augmentation principle
    d. discounting

MULTIPLE CHOICE ANSWER KEY

1. b	6. d	11. a	16. a	21. a	26. a
2. b	7. b	12. d	17. b	22. c	27. d
3. a	8. d	13. c	18. b	23. c	28. c
4. d	9. c	14. d	19. a	24. a	
5. b	10. d	15. b	20. b	25. c	

SHORT ANSWER ITEMS

1. What is the purpose of cognitive structures such as schemas, and prototypes?

2. How do cognitive structures such as schemas, prototypes, and implicit personality theories influence the encoding and recall of information about others.

3. Describe how the consistency, consensus, and distinctiveness of behavior influence our attributions of causality.

4. Describe the Fiske & Neuberg model of impression formation.

APPLICATION QUESTIONS

1. Think of a time when you first met a person and formed a very inaccurate impression. What aspects of social cognition contributed to your false impressions.

2. Describe a personal example of a schema, a script, a prototype, and an implicit personality theory.

3. Describe a personal example of each of the following: fundamental attribution error, belief in a just world, illusory correlation, and false consensus bias.

4. Think of someone you met this year and have come to know. Describe: a) your initial categorization of this person, b) any confirmatory biases you used to support this initial categorization, and c) any recategorizations or information integration that was used to modify your initial categorization.

CHAPTER FIVE

INTERPERSONAL COMMUNICATION

CHAPTER OUTLINE

The Meaning of Communication

The Channels of Communication

- Language and Paralanguage
- Gaze
- Facial Expressions
- Body Movements and Gestures
- Touch
- Interpersonal Distance
- Combining the Channels

Patterns of Communication

- Basic Dimensions of Communication
- Equilibrium and Arousal Models
- Conversational Patterns
- Conversation in Close Relationships

Deceptive Communication

- Those Lying Ways
- Detecting Deception

Communication and Social Interaction

CHAPTER REVIEW

Communication involves sending and receiving messages between people. Both parties have speaking and listening parts in the communication process. Communication occurs through a variety of channels such as language, paralanguage, facial expressions, and gestures. All channels of communication require interpretation. Even language conveys subtle messages which extend beyond the literal meaning of the words as when a friend asks "Are you busy?" when his real message is that he wants some assistance.

Paralanguage refers to how something is said. Paralanguage may convey emotion or influence our judgments of a person. Gaze may serve a variety of functions such as conveying information about liking or status, or helping to regulate turn taking in conversations. Facial expressions may express emotions. An emotion, such as fear or anger, is accompanied by a facial affect program, a specific pattern of facial muscle activity. However, we are able to partially disguise or fake facial expressions of emotion. Display rules are norms which regulate when we openly display emotion and when we try to hide our feelings.

Kinesics refers to communication through body movements including the head, legs, hands, feet, and torso. Such movements can illustrate or substitute for words and can convey information about liking and status. Touch can convey messages of friendliness, or can indicate status differences. Reactions to a casual touch may depend on the situation and the sex and status of the individuals.

Interpersonal distance varies with the nature of the interaction. We use closer distances for more personal or intimate interaction, and larger distances for more formal interaction. We maintain closer distances with those we like, and we may maintain large distances when status differences are great. When different channels provide contradictory information, we often give greatest emphasis to facial cues.

Three major dimensions seem to underlie communication: evaluation or liking, status or social control, and activity or responsiveness. Interactions between people vary in the degree of intimacy. When one person changes the intimacy level (i.e. by moving closer) the other person may make adjustments to maintain a comfortable level of intimacy (i.e., reducing gaze). The equilibrium model and the arousal model account for these adjustments. The arousal model suggests that increased intimacy can lead to either positive or negative emotions. Positive emotion leads to reciprocity (matching the increased intimacy). Negative emotion leads to attempts to reduce the level of intimacy to a comfortable level.

Conversations usually start out with a gaze and initial greetings. Persons who do not know each other well usually start talking about fairly superficial matters to establish areas of common experience. As relationships develop, people engage in self-disclosure. Self-disclosure involves revealing personal information about oneself. In most relationships, each person engages in about the same amount of self-disclosure.

Deceptive communication often differs from truthful communication in both its content and nonverbal features. Nevertheless, it is often quite difficult to accurately detect deception.

We sometimes communicate our expectations about another person (i.e., he or she is unfriendly) to that person. As a consequence of our behavior (acting in an unfriendly way), the other person confirms our beliefs (i.e., acts unfriendly). This process is called the self-fulfilling prophecy. The specific steps that cause an expectancy to be self-fulfilling are called the expectancy confirmation sequence. While self-fulfilling prophecies are common, people who are aware that another person holds negative beliefs about them may try especially hard to disprove those beliefs.

LEARNING OBJECTIVES

After completing Chapter 5, you should be able to:

1. List and describe 6 major elements of the Shannon & Weaver model of communication. (p. 116)

2. Explain how words can convey more than their dictionary meaning. (p. 118)

3. Define paralanguage and give at least 5 examples. (p. 118)

4. Describe 5 functions of gaze. (p. 119-121)

5. Explain how gaze is related to liking and to status. (p. 119-121)

6. Explain why facial expressions may correspond to emotional experiences, and why they sometimes may not. (p. 121-123)

7. Explain the purpose of a smile. (p. 123-124).

8. Explain the facial feedback hypothesis and describe some evidence for it. (p. 124)

9. Describe two types of gestures and give an example of each. (p. 125)

10. Give examples of how status differences can be reflected in body movements and gestures. (p. 126)

11. Describe differences in the way men and women respond to casual touch. (p. 126-127)

12. Describe 4 interpersonal distance zones and give an example of when each might be used. (p. 128-129)

13. Describe 3 major dimensions of communication. (p. 129-130)

14. Distinguish between compensatory and reciprocal reactions and use the arousal model to explain when each occurs. (p. 130-131)

15. Describe the communication typical of the opening, body, and closing sections of a conversation. (p. 131-133)

16. Describe aspects of the verbal content and nonverbal behavior that are more common in deceptive communications. (p. 134-135)

17. Define expectancy confirmation and explain the 5 steps in the expectancy confirmation sequence. (p. 137-138)

KEY TERMS

arousal model
communication
connotation
conversational implicature
gaze
illocution
illustrators
kinesics
locution

cooperative principle
denotation
display rules
emblems
equilibrium model
facial affect program
facial electromyography
facial feedback hypothesis
paralanguage
personal distance zone
public distance zone
self-disclosure
self-fulfilling prophecy
social distance zone
social register
visual dominance behavior

COMPLETION ITEMS

All social interaction is based on (1)______________. Interpersonal communication involves the transfer of information between a (2)______________ and a destination. Confusions or miscommunications can result because of interference or (3)______________. Communication between two people is not a one-way transfer of information, since (4)______________ parties have sending and receiving parts to play. Communication involves a number of channels including both verbal and (5)______________ channels.

The choice of words is important because each word has both a specific dictionary meaning or (6)______________ and an implicit association or (7)______________. Thus, by a poorly chosen word, we can imply things that are not meant. Sometimes a statement can convey more than the literal meaning as when a parent says "Your hair is getting long." and means "Get a haircut." A series of words conveying a literal meaning is called a (8)______________. An intended meaning which goes beyond the literal meaning is called the (9)______________. Features of a spoken message such as tone of voice, speech rate, and hesitations are called (10)______________.

Looking directly at the face of another person is called (11)______________. When we like someone, we tend to gaze at them (12)______________ than we would if we didn't like them. When people differ in status, the (13)______________ status person tends to gaze more than the other person. Mutual (14)______________ often predicts the beginning of a conversation. A high status person who wishes to exert control may, while speaking, increase the amount of gaze directed at the listener. This gaze pattern is called (15)______________ ______________ ______________.

Facial expressions can be used to recognize at least six basic (16)______________. The pattern of facial-muscle activity that accompanies a particular emotion is called a (17)______________ ______________ ______________. Facial expressions associated with a particular emotion are (18)______________ across very different cultures. Although a particular emotion may tend to trigger a particular facial expression, (19)______________ ______________ may limit the degree to which the person actually expresses the emotion.

Analysis of body movements and gestures is called (20)____________. Gestures that are directly linked to speech, such as moving the arm to emphasize a point, are called (21)______________. Gestures, such as shaking a clenched fist, which have a clear meaning even without language are termed (22)______________. If two persons are talking and one is much more relaxed, this person is probably the one with the (23)______________ status. A person who faces another, leans forward, and has a relaxed body posture probably (24)______________ the other person.

Touch may indicate a variety of things such as friendliness or differences in (25)______________. The person who initiates the touching is often thought to have (26)______________ status than the person who is touched. In many cases, women react more (27)______________ to touch than men do.

The spacing between people, or (28)______________ ______________, can communicate about the relationship between the people. The interpersonal distance zone from touching to 18 inches is termed the (29)______________ zone. Most of our interaction with acquaintances takes place in the (30)______________ ______________ zone. This zone extends from about 18 inches to (31)______________ feet. Within this zone, we tend to stand or sit (32)______________ to our friends than to casual acquaintances. Business interactions usually occur at slightly (33)______________ distances, in the (34)______________ ______________ zone. Formal interactions such as making a public speech often occur at the (35)______________ ______________ zone.

At times the various communication channels provide inconsistent messages. In such cases, people often rely more on (36)______________ cues than on other types of cues. Interpersonal communication seems to reflect three dimensions: liking or (37)______________, relative power and status or (38)______________, and responsiveness or (39)______________.

Interpersonal interactions vary in intimacy. When a person changes the level of intimacy by asking personal questions, moving closer, or gazing more, we may make adjustments to maintain our desired level of (40)______________. If a person increased intimacy by moving closer, the (41)______________ model would predict that the other person would try to restore the desired level of intimacy by doing things such as reducing gaze or turning away. Increases in intimacy are sometimes welcomed and are sometimes unwelcomed, thus the (42)______________ model suggests that we may respond to increased intimacy with either reciprocity or attempts to restore equilibrium.

In conversations, we tend to expect each person to be truthful, informative, relevant, and concise; this expectation is called the (43)______________ ______________. We interpret not only what a person literally says but what is implied, a phenomenon termed (44)______________ ______________. Thus, if we ask whether a potential blind date is attractive and are told that he or she is "real nice", we assume that he or she is not attractive.

The process of sharing feelings or personal information is called (45)______________-______________. We generally prefer that both parties in a friendship engage in relatively (46)______________ amounts of self-disclosure. Close friends engage in (47)______________ self-disclosure than casual acquaintances.

We tend to make fewer factual statements, speak with a higher pitch, and touch our face when engaging in (48)______________ communication. Because many of the cues that accompany deception are also associated with other forms of arousal such as nervousness, or fear of being incorrectly thought to be a liar, it is often (49)______________ to accurately detect deception.

At times, our initial expectation about another person may set off a sequence of events which causes the other to act in ways which confirm our belief. This process has been called the (50)_____________-_____________ _____________. The specific steps that are required for the self-fulfilling prophecy to work have been called the (51)_____________ _____________ _____________. While expectancy conformation is common, it does not (52)_____________ occur. Expectancy conformation is (53)_____________likely when person B is aware that person A holds a negative view of him or her which is inconsistent with person B's self-concept.

COMPLETION ITEM ANSWER KEY

(Answers printed in **bold type** require an exact match, but synonyms are acceptable for other items.)

1. **communication**
2. source
3. **noise**
4. both
5. **nonverbal**
6. **denotation**
7. **connotation**
8. **locution**
9. **illocution**
10. **paralanguage**
11. **gaze**
12. more
13. lower
14. **gaze**
15. **visual dominance behavior**
16. emotions
17. **facial affect program**
18. similar
19. **display rules**
20. **kinesics**
21. **illustrators**
22. **emblems**
23. higher
24. likes
25. status
26. higher
27. positively
28. **interpersonal distance**
29. **intimate**
30. **personal distance**
31. **four**
32. closer
33. greater
34. **social distance**
35. **public distance**
36. **facial**
37. **evaluation**
38. **control**
39. **activity**
40. **intimacy**
41. **equilibrium**
42. **arousal**
43. **cooperative principle**
44. **conversational implicature**
45. **self-disclosure**
46. equal
47. more
48. deceptive
49. difficult
50. **self-fulfilling prophecy**
51. **expectancy confirm-ation sequence**
52. always
53. less

MULTIPLE CHOICE ITEMS

1. A disturbance in the transmission of a communication is called:
   a. noise
   b. feedback
   c. paralanguage
   d. common ground

2. Modern views of communication suggest that:
   a. communication involves both verbal and nonverbal components
   b. the expectations of the parties shape the nature of the communication
   c. both parties have speaking and listening parts
   d. all of the above

3. Anna asks her husband if he is planning to shave today. She intends this message to mean that she wants him to shave. This interaction illustrates:
   a. paralanguage
   b. locution
   c. illocution
   d. self-disclosure

4. Through the wall, you hear the next door neighbors talking. Even though you can't understand their words, you can tell that they are arguing. This illustrates the use of:
   a. paralanguage
   b. locution
   c. illocution
   d. self-disclosure

5. Gaze can:
   a. help regulate conversation
   b. indicate status differences between individuals
   c. reflect the degree of liking between individuals
   d. all of the above

6. Which of the following statements about gaze is true?
   a. Blacks and Whites show identical patterns of gaze
   b. people look at those they dislike more than those they like
   c. the average length of a gaze is about 3 seconds
   d. in a typical, two person conversation, about 75% of the time is spent in mutual gaze

7. Which of the following is true?
   a. leaders with high visual dominance were rated highest in leadership
   b. leaders with low visual dominance were rated highest in leadership
   c. followers high in visual dominance were the best followers
   d. visual dominance involves refusing to look at the other person

8. On your world travels you notice that Italians freely express emotions such as anger and excitement while Japanese are more reserved. This difference in emotional expressiveness probably reflects cultural differences in:
   a. facial affect programs
   b. display rules
   c. locution
   d. feedback

9. Gail is mad at Mary. She doesn't say anything, but makes an obscene gesture. The gesture is an example of:
   a. an emblem
   b. a facial affect program
   c. a paralinguistic cue
   d. noise

10. The facial feedback hypothesis suggests that facial expressions of emotion:
    a. are natural reflections of our inner feelings
    b. are used to communicate feelings
    c. produce physiological effects which intensify our feelings
    d. must be learned by practice and feedback from others

11. A study in which patients were touched on the hand and arm by the nurse showed that:
    a. patients became less anxious
    b. patients became more anxious
    c. males became less anxious and females became more anxious
    d. males became more anxious and females became less anxious

12. Two friends who are having a pleasant, but casual, conversation will probably use:
    a. the public distance zone
    b. the social distance zone
    c. the personal distance zone
    d. the intimate zone

13. Which of the following situations would result in the greatest interpersonal distances:
    a. two friends having a friendly discussion
    b. a low status person approaching a high status person
    c. a high status person approaching a low status person
    d. two high status persons having a serious discussion

14. Under what circumstances would holding a pen in your mouth while looking at cartoons would increase your feelings of amusement?
    a. under no circumstances
    b. if you held the pen only in your teeth
    c. if you held the pen only in your lips
    d. only if the pen touched your tongue

15. According to the arousal model, increased intimacy on the part of another person results in:
    a. attempts to reduce the intimacy
    b. reciprocity
    c. no action
    d. either (a) or (b) depending upon the way the person labels the arousal created by the increased intimacy

16. Kim asks her friend's opinion of her new boyfriend, Jeff. The friend replies that Jeff is very smooth, meaning that he is poised and has good social skills. Kim interprets smooth to mean that the friend thinks Jeff is insincere. This confusion about the meaning of smooth illustrates the word's:
    a. social register
    b. denotation
    c. connotation
    d. feedback

17. Lanny's roommate tries to arrange a blind date. When Lanny asks about her looks, he is told that she is a nice person. Lanny concludes that she is ugly. This conclusion represents:
    a. a social register
    b. the self-fulfilling prophecy
    c. conversational implicature
    d. self-disclosure

18. Which of the following is the <u>least</u> likely to be effectively used by a perceiver to detect deception?
    a. facial expressions
    b. sweeping statements and many gaps
    c. higher pitch
    d. nervous behavior such as face touching or playing with one's glasses

19. Race differences in the use of gaze indicate that:
    a. white adults gaze more when listening than speaking, whereas black adults gaze more when speaking
    b. white adults gaze more when speaking than listening, whereas black adults gaze more when listening
    c. black children gaze more when speaking than listening, while the reverse is true of black adults
    d. black subjects tend to engage in more overall gazing than white subjects

20. Attraction can be conveyed through body movements and gestures. People who like each other are more likely to:
    a. lean forward with their bodies
    b. have direct body orientation to the other person
    c. show a more relaxed body position
    d. all of the above

21. According to Hall's categorization of interpersonal distance, smaller interpersonal distance is associated with:
    a. less liking
    b. greater liking
    c. status differences between the two people
    d. cultures in cold climates

22. Using baby talk to talk to a young child illustrates the use of a(n):
    a. social register
    b. illustrator
    c. self-fulfilling prophecy
    d. display rule

23. Mehrabian and his colleagues have found that when different communication channels provide inconsistent information, the most weight is generally given to:
    a. facial cues
    b. verbal cues
    c. vocal cues
    d. paralinguistic cues

24. Noller's research on communication between partners in a marriage suggested that:
    a. many marriages probably fail because of communication problems between the spouses
    b. women tend to be less effective than men in sending messages to their partners
    c. men are better able than women to encode positive messages, while the reverse pattern seems to hold for negative messages
    d. communication failures are more likely to be a consequence than a cause of marital problems

25. Arglye and Dean's (1965) equilibrium model of intimacy proposes that if one person's behavior in one nonverbal channel indicates more intimacy than the other wants, the latter will:
    a. reciprocate by establishing intimacy in another channel
    b. compensate by decreasing the intimacy in other channels
    c. break off the relationship
    d. launch a verbal attack

26. Research on sex differences in self-disclosure has shown that:
    a. women report more self-disclosure than men
    b. women are more likely than men to talk specifically about their relationship with their friend
    c. men and women are equally likely to talk about topical issues such as work or current events
    d. all of the above

27. People who are being deceptive:
    a. make factual statements more often
    b. avoid vague and sweeping statements
    c. frequently leave gaps in their conversation
    d. all of the above

28. When expectations produce the expected behavior, we have a(n):
    a. conversational implicature
    b. self-fulfilling prophecy
    c. cooperative principle
    d. behavioral feedback loop

MULTIPLE CHOICE ANSWER KEY

1. a	6. c	11. d	16. c	21. b	26. d
2. d	7. a	12. c	17. c	22. a	27. c
3. c	8. b	13. b	18. a	23. a	28. b
4. a	9. a	14. b	19. a	24. d	
5. d	10. c	15. d	20. d	25. b	

SHORT ANSWER ITEMS

1. List and briefly describe seven channels of communication.

2. Explain how the expectations and understandings of both persons engaged in a conversation affect communication, and why it is necessary to establish common understandings.

3. Describe the five steps in the expectancy confirmation sequence.

4. Describe three major dimensions of communicative behavior.

5. How is nonverbal behavior used to regulate conversation?

APPLICATION QUESTIONS

1. Describe a time when you gave or received a communication in which the locution differed from the illocution.

2. Give an example of a time when the paralinguistic cues lead to a different understanding than was conveyed by the verbal message.

3. Give a personal example of how gaze was used to indicate liking or status.

4. Describe how your perceptions of a person were influenced by the person's body movements or gestures.

5. Describe three times when you were casually touched. For each instance, describe the feelings or impressions created by the touch.

6. Give an example of a time when you used each of Hall's four interpersonal distance zones.

7. Describe a personal example of the operation of a self-fulfilling prophecy.

CHAPTER SIX

THE NATURE OF ATTITUDES

CHAPTER OUTLINE

The History of Attitudes

- Definitions of Attitudes
- Components of Attitudes
- Measurement of Attitudes

The Formation of Attitudes

- Direct Experience With the Attitude Object
- Parents and Peer Groups
- Media Influence

The Structure and Functions of Attitudes

- Complexity and Values
- How Attitudes Interrelate
- Attitudes and Information

Attitudes and Behavior

- What Attitude and What Behavior?
- A Theory of Planned Behavior
- How Do Attitudes Influence Behavior?
- Reason versus Spontaneity

CHAPTER REVIEW

Attitudes represents our thoughts and feelings about issues, people, and objects and often predict our behavior. Attitudes include cognitive components which deal with our beliefs, and affective components which deal with our feelings. Attitudes are mental states or constructs and, thus, cannot be directly observed. However, attitudes are often measured by rating scales such as Likert scales or the semantic differential technique.

Attitudes are acquired in many ways. We may form attitudes by direct experience, from others such as our parents or peers, and from mass media. Principles of classical and operant conditioning influence the formation of attitudes.

Attitudes on various topics are often interrelated and seem to be organized into a cognitive system. Values (such as equality, freedom, or practicality) or the general way a person views the world may influence attitudes on several issues. A person's attitudes may influence the way he or she attends to, interprets, and remembers information. Attitudes about an issue may be simple and unipolar, reflecting clear cut views on the issue. Other attitudes may be more complex bipolar attitudes reflecting somewhat mixed feelings about the issue.

Attitudes and behavior do not always correspond. Situational pressures sometimes make it difficult for us to act as we wish. Furthermore, several attitudes may be relevant to a given behavior. The theory of planned action suggests that our behavior is influenced by our attitude toward engaging in that behavior and our beliefs about other people's reactions to such behavior. When we are motivated and have the opportunity to give careful thought to our behavior, our behavior is based on planned action involving the careful analysis of our attitudes and subjective norms. At other times, we seem to base our behavior on spontaneous processing which emphasizes the particular attitudes that are most salient to us at the moment. Thus, our attitudes influence our behavior, but sometimes they do so in a spontaneous manner based on only superficial thought, and sometimes the influence of attitudes is based on careful planning.

LEARNING OBJECTIVES

After completing this chapter, you should be able to:

1. Define attitude. (p. 144)

2. Describe the two essential components of an attitude. (p. 145)

3. Describe two types of attitude scales. (p. 146).

4. Describe two indirect techniques for measuring attitudes. (p. 147)

5. Explain the process of classical conditioning of attitudes. (p. 148)

6. Explain how reinforcement and social learning can lead to the formation of attitudes. (p. 149-150)

7. Explain how value pluralism and the variety of knowledge contribute to attitudinal complexity. (p. 151-152)

8. Explain how selective exposure serves to maintain current attitudes. (p. 154)

9. Describe how the specificity and generality of attitude measurement relate to the prediction of behavior. (p. 155-156)

10. Describe the major components of the theory of planned action. (p. 156-158).

11. Explain why attitude accessibility affects behavior. (p. 158-159).

12. Describe three things which make an attitude more accessible. (p. 158-159)

13. Distinguish between spontaneous processing and planned action. (p. 156-161)

14. Describe two factors which determine whether persons engage in spontaneous processing or planned action. (p. 160-161)

KEY TERMS

affective component
attitude
behavioral component
behavioral intention
bipolar attitude
classical conditioning
cognitive component
CR
CS
demand characteristics
evaluation apprehension
fear of invalidity
lost-letter procedure
Likert scale
MODE
priming
schematic function of attitudes
semantic differential technique
selective exposure
self-perception theory
social learning theory
subjective norm
theory of planned behavior
unipolar attitude
UCS
value
world view

COMPLETION ITEMS

An (1)_______________ is a construct that represents a person's thoughts, and feelings about an object, issue, or person. While an (2)_______________ has a specific object or focus, (3)_______________ are broad abstract goals such as bravery or honesty. Attitudes have two basic components. The (4)_______________ component deals with beliefs and ideas a person has about some object, while the (5)_______________ component deals with emotions or feelings.

Since attitudes are constructs, they cannot be directly observed, and must be (6)_______________. One way to determine a person's attitude is to ask him or her. A popular procedure for assessing attitudes involves asking person's to indicate how much they agree or disagree with a series of statements about an object. This method uses a type of scale called a (7)_______________ _______________. A technique of asking persons to rate an object on several scales (such as good/bad or fair/unfair) is called the (8)_______________ _______________ technique. A concern about whether one is making a good impression is called (9)_______________ _______________. Evaluation apprehension sometimes causes persons to give distorted responses to attitude scales. Another approach to attitude measurement is to infer attitudes from behavior as in the (10)_______________ - _______________ _______________ where the experimenter observes the number of postcards that are mailed to different organizations.

Attitudes are formed through direct (11)_______________, through influence from (12)_______________, and from mass media. Sometimes a person forms an attitude by association of the object with something positive or negative, as when a particular religious group is repeatedly described with negative terms. In such instances, the attitude toward the religious group was formed through the process of (13)_____________ _____________. Principles of operant reinforcement may explain how (14)_________________ such as approval from others may strengthen attitudes. Attitude formation by imitation of others is emphasized by (15)_______________ _______________ theory.

People vary in the extent to which they have complex, multidimensional attitudes which integrate at a variety of information. Persons with highly complex attitudes are (16)_______________ extreme in their positions than persons holding simpler views on the issue. Some issues involve a conflict of values such as economic growth and environmental protection. (17)_______________ _______________ refers to situations in which the people give relatively equal weight to potentially conflicting values. In such cases, the attitudes may be complex. An attitude for which the person has information that supports his or her position, but also knows things that tend not to fit with the position is called a (18)_______________ attitude. A (19)_______________ attitude contains only knowledge that supports one's evaluation.

Our attitudes may influence the processing of information. We are more likely to remember information that is (20)______________ with our attitudes and to interpret new information in ways that are consistent with our (21)_______________. At times, we may make special efforts to look for information which supports our beliefs and avoid contradictory information. Such efforts illustrate (22)_______________ _______________.

Fishbein and Ajzen have developed a theory to explain the relationships between attitudes and behavior, the theory of (23)_______________ _______________. In this model, a person's attitude about engaging in a specific behavior depends on the person's beliefs about the (24)______________ of the behavior and his or her (25)______________ of those outcomes. The model also deals with the person's beliefs about what others think he or she should do. This component is called (26)______________ ______________. Since it is unlikely that one will exert much effort which he or she thinks is useless, the model emphasizes the importance of perceived behavioral (27)______________. Together, a person's attitude toward the behavior, subjective norms, and perceived behavior control determine his or her (28)______________ to perform the behavior.

At times we may not be actively aware of a particular attitude, but an attitude may be made accessible by cues from the environment. Attitudes that are very important to us are usually (29)______________. Sometimes we infer our attitudes by reflecting upon our behavior as is suggested by (30)______________-______________ theory. Attitudes that are important to us, have been expressed often, or have been made accessible are more likely to guide our (31)______________.

On some occasions, we may carefully evaluate the reasons for our behavior as suggested by the theory of (32)______________ ______________. On other occasions, when we give little thought to our behavior and base our behavior on whatever attitudes are most accessible, we engage in (33)______________ processing. Engaging in planned rather than spontaneous processing seems to require both the (34)______________ and (35)______________ to do so.

COMPLETION ITEM ANSWER KEY

(Answers printed in **bold type** require an exact match, but synonyms are acceptable for other items.)

1. **attitude**
2. **attitude**
3. **values**
4. **cognitive** (or **knowledge**)
5. **affective** (or **evaluative**)
6. inferred
7. **Likert scale**
17. **value pluralism**
18. **bipolar**
19. **unipolar**
20. consistent
21. **attitudes**
22. **selective exposure**
23. **planned behavior**
24. consequences
25. evaluation

8. **semantic differential**
9. **evaluation apprehension**
10. **lost-letter procedure**
11. experience
12. others
13. **classical conditioning**
14. reinforcements
15. **social learning**
16. less

26. **subjective norms**
27. control
28. intention
29. accessible
30. **self-perception**
31. behavior
32. **planned behavior**
33. **spontaneous**
34. motivation
35. opportunity

MULTIPLE CHOICE ITEMS

1. Asking persons to indicate the extent to which they agree or disagree with a series of statements about a topic such as the president's performance illustrates the use of:
   a. the semantic differential
   b. a Likert scale
   c. the lost-letter procedure
   d. all of the above

2. Rating a topic (such as marijuana) on a series of dimensions (such as good-bad, useful-useless, etc.) illustrates attitude measurement using the:
   a. semantic differential
   b. Likert scale
   c. lost-letter procedure
   d. all of the above

3. How are attitudes formed?
   a. on the basis of our personal experience with the object
   b. through influence from our parents and friends
   c. through influence from the media
   d. all of the above

4. Little Stevie notices that Michael Jordan wears Nike shoes and concludes that these must be super shoes. Stevie's formation of the favorable attitude toward the shoes illustrates attitude formation through:
   a. personal experience
   b. direct reinforcement
   c. imitation
   d. all of the above

5. Alice learns that her new roommate is from New York. She has never met anyone from New York, but has heard words like rude and pushy associated with New Yorkers. As a result Alice forms a negative attitude about her new roommate through the process of:
   a. classical conditioning
   b. direct reinforcement
   c. personal experience
   d. semantic differential

6. If the media strongly emphasize a particular political issue such as arms control policy, it is likely that viewers will:
   a. ignore the issue when making evaluations of politicians
   b. use the issue in evaluations of politicians
   c. become bored with politics
   d. ignore all other issues

7. Persons with complex political beliefs tend to be:
   a. extreme liberals
   b. extreme conservatives
   c. moderate
   d. power hungry

8. Persons committed to high technology, economic growth and quantitative decision-making would be classified as endorsing:
   a. a theory of planned action
   b. world view A
   c. world view B
   d. the semantic differential

9. Dick is an avid hunter and owns many handguns. He is opposed to any type of gun control legislation. Whenever he sees an article against gun control, he reads it carefully, but he avoids any article supporting gun control. His behavior illustrates:
   a. self-perception
   b. salience
   c. selective exposure
   d. classical conditioning

10. Which of the following statements best reflect the relationship between attitudes and behavior?
    a. behavior always corresponds to attitudes
    b. general, overall assessments of attitudes are excellent predictors of specific behavior
    c. there may be a close relationship between specific attitudes and corresponding behavior
    d. there is little, if any, relationship between attitudes and behavior

11. Attitudes may not always match behavior because:
    a. situational pressures may cause a person to act in a particular way regardless of his or her attitudes
    b. several attitudes may be relevant to a given behavior
    c. an attitude may not be readily accessible
    d. all of the above

12. Sylvia wants to move in with her boyfriend, but doesn't because she knows her family and friends would not approve. Her desire to move in with her boyfriend reflects a(n):
    a. attitude toward the behavior
    b. subjective norm
    c. intention
    d. behavioral control

13. In the example above, Sylvia's reluctance to live with her boyfriend was a result of:
    a. a lack of behavioral control
    b. subjective norms
    c. behavioral intention
    d. planned action

14. According to the theory of planned action, behavior is best predicted by:
    a. the attitude toward the behavior
    b. subjective norms
    c. intention
    d. beliefs about control

15. Attitudes are more likely to be accessible when:
    a. people are young
    b. the attitudes are weak
    c. the attitudes have been expressed rarely
    d. environmental cues cause the person to think about the topic of the attitude

16. Chester likes the president, thinks he is a real statesman, and voted for him. These statements reflect respectively the:
    a. behavioral, cognitive and affective components
    b. affective, cognitive and behavioral components
    c. affective, behavioral and cognitive
    d. cognitive, affective, behavioral

17. Which of the following techniques of attitude measurement is not subject to problems associated with self-reports:
    a. semantic differential
    b. Likert scale
    c. open-ended questions
    d. the lost-letter procedure

18. The study of student's attitudes about "Aloha week" illustrates attitude formation and change through:
    a. the mass media
    b. operant reinforcement
    c. classical conditioning
    d. personal experience

19. Broad abstract goals that lack a specific object or referent point are called:
    a. constructs
    b. attitudes
    c. values
    d. opinions

20. A person who loves Jeeps, and thinks they are great automobiles has:
    a. an attitude
    b. a value
    c. a subjective norm
    d. evaluation apprehension

21. Values:
    a. are more specific than attitudes
    b. are identical to attitudes
    c. may influence attitudes
    d. are identical to opinions

22. Each day, Carissa comes home from work and casually turns to the television network news on the usual channel. Her choice of a channel can best be explained by:
    a. the theory of planned action
    b. spontaneous processing
    c. social learning
    d. demand characteristics

23. Assessing attitudes through the use of open-ended questions has the disadvantage of:
    a. eliciting a broad range of viewpoints
    b. low reliability
    c. difficulty of comparing respondents' answers
    d. (b) and (c)

24. LaPierre (1934), who toured the U. S. with a Chinese couple, found that people's attitudes and behavior toward Chinese:
    a. didn't match
    b. were highly similar
    c. were both strongly negative
    d. (b) and (c)

25. The theory of planned action includes:
    a. the person's attitude toward the action
    b. spontaneous processing
    c. the accessibility of the attitude
    d. the complexity of the attitude

26. Our behavior is likely to be based on planned action rather than spontaneous processing:
    a. never
    b. always
    c. when the costs of incorrect behavior are high and we have sufficient time
    d. when we are among friends

MULTIPLE CHOICE ANSWER KEY

1. b	6. b	11. d	16. b	21. c	26. c
2. a	7. c	12. a	17. d	22. b	
3. d	8. b	13. b	18. b	23. d	
4. c	9. c	14. c	19. c	24. a	
5. a	10. c	15. d	20. a	25. a	

SHORT ANSWER ITEMS

1. Distinguish between an attitude and a value.

2. How are attitudes formed?

3. Distinguish between planned and spontaneous processing.

4. Describe the theory of planned action.

5. What is meant by the statement: attitudes are constructs?

6. What is a Likert scale?

APPLICATION QUESTIONS

1. Take a particular attitude you hold (such as your attitude toward abortion, nuclear disarmament, or drug testing) and:
   a. Describe the cognitive, and affective components of that attitude.

b. Explain how the attitude was formed.

c. Using the theory of planned action, explain why your behavior may or may not correspond with your attitude.

CHAPTER SEVEN

PERSUASION AND ATTITUDE CHANGE

CHAPTER OUTLINE

Theories of Attitude Change

- Social Judgment Theory
- Balance Theory
- Cognitive Dissonance Theory
- Functional Theories

The Process of Attitude Change

- Sequential Models
- Parallel Models

Elements of Persuasion

- Source
- Message
- Context
- Recipient

Resistance to Persuasion

- Anticipatory Attitude Change
- Reactance
- Inoculation

CHAPTER REVIEW

A variety of theories of attitude change exist. Social judgment theory suggests that we compare a message to our current beliefs. Messages that are very discrepant from our initial attitudes are rejected, while messages with moderate discrepancy may result in attitude change.

Balance theory deals with our preference for cognitive consistency. For example, it is uncomfortable (unbalanced) to believe that your friend disagrees with you on an important issue. Changing your attitude about either the friend or the issue would restore balance.

Cognitive dissonance theory suggests that we experience tension (dissonance) when our beliefs and actions are incompatible. When we perceive ourselves as responsible for actions which produce aversive consequences, we are likely to experience dissonance. Dissonance may cause a person to change his or her attitude to bring it in line with behavior.

Functional theories note that persons hold attitudes for a variety of reasons. These include attitudes held to organize knowledge, those held to enhance self-esteem, and those held for other reasons.

The process of attitude change can be broken down into three steps: attention, comprehension, and acceptance. All are required for attitude change. When an issue is of some importance to a person, he or she may engage in central processing and carefully consider the evidence. At other times, we engage in peripheral processing and make decisions with less thought. Peripheral processing may involve the use of heuristics or simple decision rules such as "listen to the expert" or "don't believe an unlikable person".

The degree of attitude change depends upon the source of the communication, the nature of the message, the context, and the nature of the person receiving the message. Sources high in credibility produce greater attitude change. Specific factors such as expertise, trustworthiness, attractiveness and similarity to the recipient can affect attitude change.

Messages that arouse fear are sometimes used to change attitudes. Fear arousing appeals seem to be effective if the feared consequence is unpleasant, the event is likely to happen if the recommended action is not taken, and the person feels capable of taking effective action.

Most issues have two sides. Presenting only one side may work well when the audience is friendly to your position, when your position is the only one that will be heard, or that you desire only temporary attitude change.

Otherwise, a two sided message produces greater attitude change. If two sides of an issue are presented, order of presentation may influence the relative impact of the two messages. The nature of the influence depends upon the timing of the messages and the attitude measurement. A written message may lead to greater comprehension of difficult material, while a live or videotaped presentation may result in less systematic analysis and greater reliance on heuristics.

Distractions interfere with our ability to carefully think about a message. Thus, distraction may prevent systematic processing and increase the chances of heuristic processing.

Intelligent people are not likely to be influenced by unsupported arguments, but are influenced by complex messages. Persons high in self-monitoring are more responsive to image-oriented messages while low self-monitors are more influenced by the substance of the message.

Just as a vaccination protects one from later exposure to a disease, prior exposure and refutation of arguments for the other side of an issue can serve as an inoculation that makes one more resistant to persuasion. Reactance suggests that we will sometimes resist persuasion in an attempt to demonstrate our sense of control.

LEARNING OBJECTIVES

After completing this chapter, you should be able to:

1. Describe how the extent of attitude change is dependent upon the discrepancy between a person's position on an issue and a message designed to change the attitude. (p. 165-167)

2. Explain balance theory's predictions concerning attitude change. (p. 167-169)

3. Distinguished between balanced and unbalanced states. (p. 168)

4. Define cognitive dissonance, and explain how it can lead to attitude change. (p. 169-174)

5. Describe two conditions that are necessary for the arousal of dissonance. (p. 171)

6. List and explain five functions that attitudes may serve. (p. 174-176).

7. Describe three sequential steps that are required for attitude change. (p. 176)

8. Distinguish between central and peripheral processing. (p. 177-178)

9. Describe at least five factors which make central processing more likely. (p. 177)

10. Explain how the use of heuristics can influence attitude change. (p. 178-179).

11. Describe four characteristics of a person which can affect their persuasiveness. (p. 180-181)

12. Explain when fear appeals are likely to stimulate attitude change. (p. 181-183)

13. Explain when two-sided messages are most effective and when one-sided messages are most effective. (p. 183)

14. Describe primacy and recency effects, and explain when each is likely to occur. (p. 183-184).

15. Explain how personality traits such as intelligence and self-monitoring affect a person's reactions to persuasive appeals. (p. 185-186)

16. Explain the concept of reactance and how it affects attitude change. (p. 187-188)

17. Define inoculation and explain its role in resistance to persuasion. (p. 188-189)

KEY TERMS

anchor
anticipatory attitude change
assimilation effect
balance theory
central processing
cognitive dissonance
contrast effect
ego-defensive function
elaboration likelihood model
functional theory
heuristic
inoculation
instrumentality function
knowledge function
latitude of acceptance
latitude of noncommitment
latitude of rejection
one-sided communication
peripheral processing
reactance
selective exposure
self-affirmation
self-monitoring
self-perception theory
social adjustment function
social judgment theory
two-sided communication
value expressive function

COMPLETION ITEMS

According to social judgment theory, our own attitude serves as an(1) ______________ which we use to judge messages. A (2)______________ ______________ occurs when we distort a message that is quite different from our belief and perceive it as being even more different. A shift in judgment toward the anchor point is likely when a message is very (3)_____________ to our attitude. This effect is called an (4)______________ ______________. The concept of (5)______________ ____ ______________ emphasizes that an attitude consists of a range of acceptable positions. Messages which are so extreme that they are quickly rejected fall within the (6)______________ ____ ______________. Messages that fall between the latitudes of acceptance and rejection are in the (7)______________ _____ ____________.

Heider's (8)______________ theory suggests that we like to keep relevant attitudes consistent with each other. If you find that your friend favors communism and you despise communism, then your attitudes are (9)______________. You could restore (10)______________ by changing your (11)______________ about communism or about your friend.

According to Festinger's theory, when two cognitions contradict each other a person experiences (12)______________ ____________. Acting inconsistently with one's beliefs might produce dissonance if the behavior has (13)______________ consequences and if the person accepts (14)______________ responsibility for the action. Dissonance may result in (15)______________ change.

The (16)______________ theory holds that people hold attitudes for a variety of reasons. For example, a person may hold an attitude because it serves to organize information; thus, the attitude would have a (17)______________ function. A person who looks down on a variety of ethnic and religious minorities might do so to preserve his or her self-esteem, illustrating the (18)______________-______________ function.

Sometimes people change their attitudes by systematically evaluating information and rationally choose which attitude is best. This type of evaluation reflects (19)______________ processing. At other times, people are less careful about attitude change. We sometimes use mental shortcuts called (20)______________ to quickly evaluate a message. Automatically dismissing what a salesperson tells you would illustrate your use of a (21)______________. Attitude change in which little thought and analysis is given to the argument, as when the person is influenced by the attractiveness of the source, or by the use of heuristics represents (22)______________ ______________.

Hovland's sequential model of attitude change suggests that attitude change requires three steps. The steps are (23)______________, (24)______________, and (25)______________. The person who initiates a persuasive message is called the (26)______________. The credibility of the source is determined by factors such as expertise, (27)______________, attractiveness, and similarity. Messages which do <u>not</u> serve the communicator's self-interest are (28)______________ credible than self-serving messages. People who are attractive may be (29)______________ persuasive than a less attractive source.

Showing graphic pictures of bodies mutilated in a traffic accident while urging people not to drive drunk is an example of a (30)____________ ______________. Fear appeals are more effective when the potential harm is (31)______________, the threatened event is likely, and the recommended action is perceived as (32)______________.

A message which presents one side of the issue, but also acknowledges and tries to refute the other side of the issue is called a (33)______________-______________ communication. If you are trying to convince a relatively friendly audience who is unlikely to be aware or hear arguments from the other side, then a (34)______________-______________ communication is appropriate. When two sides of an issue are presented the order of presentation may effect the relative impact of the two sides.

(35)______________ processing is more likely with a written message, while a face-to-face or a videotaped message is more likely to result in (36)______________ processing. A (37)______________ interferes with the person's ability to critically analyze the message, thus, distraction will (38)______________ the chances of central processing. (39)______________ not only serves as distraction, it also provides information that contradicts the message. Thus, a heckler often (40)______________ the persuasiveness of the message. However, a speaker who calmly and relevantly responds to the heckler may (41)______________ the negative effects of heckling.

Persons of high intelligence are (42)______________ influenced by complex messages than by messages that are unsupported. Persons high in (43)______________-______________ are more likely to be influenced by image-oriented advertisements. Low self-monitors are (44)______________ influenced by advertisements stressing quality than advertisements stressing image. Compared to women, men are (45)______________ likely to change their attitudes.

People respond in a variety of ways to persuasive attempts. We sometimes change our attitudes readily, and at other times, resist attitude change. At times, people seem to change their attitudes in the direction of a persuasive message, even before the message is presented, thus showing (46)____________ ______________ ______________. Such change is most likely when the person is (47)______________ personally involved with the issue, and may simply be a from of impression management rather than (48)______________ attitude change. In other instances, warning a person that a persuasive attempt will be made often arouses (49)______________ . When this occurs, attitude change is (50)_______________ likely.

COMPLETION ITEM ANSWER KEY

(Answere printed in **bold type** require an exact match, but synonyms are acceptable for other items.)

1. **anchor**
2. **contrast effect**
3. similar
4. **assimilation effect**
5. **latitude of acceptance**
6. **latitude of rejection**
7. **latitude of noncommitment**
8. **balance**
9. **unbalanced**
10. **balance**
11. **attitude**
12. **cognitive dissonance**
13. aversive
14. personal
15. attitude
16. **functional**
17. **knowledge**
18. **ego-defensive**
19. **central**
20. **heuristics**
21. **heuristic**
22. **peripheral processing**
23. **attention**
24. **comprehension**
25. **acceptance**
26. **source**
27. trustworthiness
28. more
29. more
30. **fear appeal**
31. great
32. effective
33. **two-sided**
34. **one-sided**
35. **central**
36. **peripheral**
37. distraction
38. decrease
39. **heckling**
40. decrease
41. overcome
42. more
43. **self-monitoring**
44. more
45. equally
46. **anticipatory attitude change**
47. not
48. real
49. **reactance**
50. not

MULTIPLE CHOICE ITEMS

1. Attempts to change our attitudes are most likely to come from:
   a. our immediate family
   b. causal acquaintances
   c. sales persons
   d. politicians

2. Which of the following types of people are more likely to be influenced by emotional, image-oriented advertisements than by advertisements stressing rational arguments.
   a. highly intelligent people
   b. people with high self-esteem
   c. high self-monitors
   d. women

3. Julie finds the car of her dreams but wants to see if another dealer will give her a better price on the same model. The salesman tries to convince her to buy now and tells her someone else has been looking at the car and may return later in the day to buy it. She disregards his information because she thinks he is just pressuring her so he won't lose a sale. He is not persuasive because of a lack of perceived:
   a. knowledge
   b. trustworthiness
   c. attractiveness
   d. similarity

4. Barbara is wanting to buy a computer. Her friend Linda who knows little about computers recommends one brand, but her friend Audrey who is a top level computer programmer recommends another brand. Barbara is convinced by Audrey because of greater:
   a. expertise
   b. trustworthiness
   c. attractiveness
   d. similarity

5. A fear appeal is more likely to be successful if:
   a. the feared event is really awful
   b. the feared event is very likely if the recommended action isn't taken
   c. the recommended action is considered very effective
   d. all of the above

6. Steve's parents unsuccessfully use fear appeals to try to get him not to buy a motorcycle. The failure of the fear appeal is most likely due to:
   a. a lack of credibility of the source
   b. the feared event isn't really very bad
   c. the feared event isn't considered likely
   d. he has low self-efficacy

7. Alex hears messages dealing with two sides of an issue. Both messages are equal in persuasiveness. He hears the first message one day, hears the second message a week later, and is immediately asked about his attitude. Which message will have the greatest impact?
   a. the first message
   b. the second message
   c. they will have equal impact
   d. neither message will have an impact

8. If Alex hears message 1 immediately followed by message 2, and two weeks later is asked about his attitude, which message will have the greatest impact?
   a. the first message
   b. the second message
   c. they will have equal impact
   d. neither message will have an impact

9. Pamphlets promoting breast self-examinations were more successful if they :
   a. cited female doctors rather than male doctors
   b. pictured pretty women rather than unattractive women
   c. stressed dangers of failure to conduct self-examinations
   d. stressed the positive consequences of self-examinations

10. Highly intelligent people are:
    a. less likely to change their attitudes
    b. more likely to change their attitudes
    c. less likely to be influenced by weak, unsupported arguments
    d. more likely to be persuaded by image-oriented messages

11. When a person is using central processing, he or she is likely to:
    a. use heuristics
    b. use peripheral processing
    c. engage in careful, systematic thinking
    d. be influenced by face-to-face messages, but not written messages

12. When a person receives a persuasive communication, his or her own opinion serves as a(n):
    a. anchor
    b. heuristic
    c. balance point
    d. contrast effect

13. According to social judgment theory, if a person is presented with a message that is extremely different from his or her initial attitude, he or she will:
    a. change their attitude
    b. reject the message and maintain the initial attitude
    c. engage in central processing
    d. show an assimilation effect

14. Brenda dislikes Hal. Brenda loves rock music, and Hal hates rock music. Brenda's attitudes are in a _____ state.
    a. dissonant
    b. balanced
    c. unbalanced
    d. peripheral

15. Cognitive dissonance:
    a. is an uncomfortable state
    b. is likely to occur when two of a person's cognitions contradict each other
    c. may lead to attitude change
    d. all of the above

16. Gail believes that casual sex is bad, but while on vacation she meets a charming man and goes wild. Because her behavior and her attitudes are inconsistent, she experiences guilt and tension and eventually decides that casual sex is not so bad. Her attitude change can best be explained by:
    a. social judgment theory
    b. cognitive dissonance theory
    c. functional theory
    d. peripheral processing

17. Danny is afraid of snakes and goes to a clinic to cure this fear. There he is asked to go through a very demanding and stressful therapy program. As a result, he becomes more committed to overcoming his fear of snakes. Danny's experience can best be explained by:
    a. social judgment theory
    b. balance theory
    c. cognitive dissonance theory
    d. functional theory

18. We are most likely to be influenced by a source, or communicator, who is:
    a. expert
    b. trustworthy
    c. arguing against his or her own interest
    d. all of the above

19. A one-sided argument works best when:
    a. the audience initially agrees with you
    b. someone else will present the other side
    c. you want long-lasting attitude change
    d. (b) and (c)

20. Which of the following statements about personality and ease of persuasion is true?
    a. women are easier to persuade than men
    b. intelligent people are harder to persuade than less intelligent people
    c. people low in self-esteem are easier to persuade than those high in self-esteem
    d. none of the above

21. According to social judgment theory, the discrepancy between a persuasive communication and the recipient's own attitude is related to amount of attitude change in what way?
    a. linear, the most discrepant communications produce the most change
    b. linear, the least discrepant communications produce the most change
    c. curvilinear, moderately discrepant communications produce the most change
    d. by a U-shaped function, the most extreme and least extreme communications produce the most change

22. According to cognitive consistency theories such as balance theory and cognitive dissonance theory, holding inconsistent attitudes:
    a. is uncomfortable
    b. may lead to attitude change
    c. is only a problem for unintelligent individuals
    d. (a) and (b)

23. You find that you and your friend both agree in disliking a certain campus political group. According to Heider's balance theory, this situation is:
    a. balanced
    b. unbalanced
    c. dissonant
    d. unstable

24. According to dissonance theory, after considering two different types of cars and purchasing one, you will:
    a. like the one you bought less than you did before you bought it
    b. like the one you bought more than you did before you bought it
    c. like the one you didn't buy more than the one you bought
    d. try to find out all you can about both cars

25. Paying someone to argue against his or her own beliefs can produce attitude change if:
    a. the individual does not feel personally responsible for the argument
    b. the person had little perceived choice about making the argument
    c. there is little pay
    d. the argument is not very convincing

26. According to functional theory, our attempts to change a person's attitude are more likely to be successful if we:
    a. determine what needs are met by the attitude
    b. reinforce the new attitude and punish the old one
    c. give many arguments in the latitude of acceptance
    d. offer small incentives

27. Attitudes serving the value expressive function, help the person to:
    a. have a positive attitude toward something that is useful in meeting his or her needs
    b. allow the person to protect his or her self-esteem
    c. give meaning to a chaotic world
    d. express aspects of his or her self-concept

28. Research concerning inoculation suggests that the best way to protect someone against an attack on his or her position on an issue is to provide:
    a. additional supportive arguments
    b. no warning of the forthcoming attack
    c. refuted counterarguments
    d. a direct attack

29. Choosing a political candidate because of the political party affiliation rather than carefully considering the positions of the candidates illustrates the use of:
    a. reactance
    b. inoculation
    c. central processing
    d. a heuristic

30. Which type of advertisement results in the greatest amount of attitude change?
    a. a rational advertisement
    b. an emotional advertisement
    c. which type of advertisement is more effective depends on the reasons for the person's current attitude
    d. the two types of advertisements are equally effective for all people

MULTIPLE CHOICE ANSWER KEY

1. a	6. c	11. c	16. b	21. c	26. a
2. c	7. b	12. a	17. c	22. d	27. d
3. b	8. a	13. b	18. d	23. a	28. c
4. a	9. c	14. b	19. a	24. b	29. d
5. d	10. c	15. d	20. d	25. c	30. c

SHORT ANSWER ITEMS

1. Describe three basis steps required for attitude change.

2. How can characteristics of the source of a communication influence the amount of attitude change?

3. When would it be best to use two-sided arguments?

4. When two sides of a message are presented, how does the timing of the messages and the attitude measurement effect the relative impact of the first and second messages?

5. How is the amount of discrepancy between a person's initial position and the message related to attitude change?

6. What is cognitive dissonance, and when is a person likely to experience it?

7. Distinguish between central and peripheral processing. When is each most likely to occur?

APPLICATION QUESTIONS

1. Think of a situation where you would like to change a particular person's attitude about a particular topic. Use your knowledge of the effects of the source, message, context, and recipient to design an effective attitude change strategy.

2. Describe three times when you experienced cognitive dissonance.

3. Attitudes may serve five functions. For at least four of these functions, think of an attitude of yours that serves that function.

4. Describe a time when you used central processing and a time when you used peripheral processing.

5. Describe four heuristics that you have used when faced with a persuasive message.

CHAPTER EIGHT

SOCIAL INFLUENCE AND PERSONAL CONTROL

CHAPTER OUTLINE

CHAPTER REVIEW

This chapter deals with the extent to which our behavior is influenced or controlled by others, and our feelings about control and a lack of control. Conformity is the yielding to group pressure when no request is made to do so. Conformity is caused by informational influence (as when the behavior of others implies that their behavior is correct) and normative influence (a desire to fit in with the group). The extent of conformity varies with a variety of personal factors (ego strength, intellectual effectiveness, inferiority feelings, etc.) and a variety of situational factors (size of group, extent of agreement, amount of discrepancy, etc.)

Compliance involves yielding to a direct request. The foot-in-the-door effect demonstrates that compliance with a small request increases compliance with a subsequent large request. The foot-in-the-door effect may occur because compliance with the first request may influence a person's self-perception. Following a very large request (which is refused) with a smaller request increases compliance with the smaller request, illustrating the door-in-the-face effect. This effect occurs because the second request is seen as a concession, and the person feels obligated to agree with this scaled-down request. The low-ball and lure procedures involve getting agreement, then shifting the terms of the agreement.

Power involves the ability to get others to comply. Power may be derived from any of five bases: coercive power (ability to punish), reward power, expert power (superior knowledge), legitimate power (authority to make requests), and referent power (identification). Compliance with an order from someone in authority is called obedience. Milgram's famous shock experiment illustrated that pressures to be obedient can result in extreme compliance.

We generally like to feel that we are in control of events that affect us, and sometimes overestimate our ability to determine the course of events. Belief that we have control can improve performance, and improve happiness. People experience psychological reactance when they feel their freedom has been limited. We may take action to restore that freedom as when a person does something just because another person says he or she is not allowed to do it. When people experience repeated instances of lack of control, they may develop a state of learned helplessness, a belief that they cannot control what happens to them. Learned helplessness can cause people to quit trying, fail to learn from experience, become depressed, and loose self-esteem.

LEARNING OBJECTIVES

After completing Chapter 8, you should be able to:

1. Define conformity. (p. 194)
2. Distinguish between informational and normative social influence. (p. 195-196)
3. Explain how self-categorization can lead to conformity. (p. 196)
4. Distinguish between independence and anticonformity. (p. 196-197)
5. Describe the effect of group membership on both conformity and anticonformity. (p. 197)
6. Distinguish between compliance and conformity. (p. 199)
7. Describe the foot-in-the-door effect, and explain why it occurs. (199-200)
8. Describe the door-in-the-face effect, and explain why it occurs. (p. 200-201).
9. Describe the low-ball procedure, and explain how it operates. (p. 201-202)
10. Describe the lure and explain why it works. (p. 202-203)

11. Discuss how concerns about politeness and saving face can affect the choice of strategies to gain compliance. (p. 203-204)

12. List and describe the five forms of power identified by French and Raven. (p. 204-205)

13. Explain how a person's explanation of their compliance may depend upon which form of power is used to obtain compliance. (p. 205)

14. Describe the basic finding of Milgram's studies of obedience. (p.206-208)

15. Discuss the ethical concerns raised by the Milgram studies. (p. 208-209)

16. Describe and give an example to illustrate the illusion of control. (p. 210-211)

17. Discuss how perceptions of control differ for positive and negative events and recurring and nonrecurring events.
(p. 211)

18. Describe why it is important to maintain a belief in control. (p. 212).

19. Distinguish between an internal and an external locus of control. (p. 213).

20. Describe how reactance affects a person's reaction to attempted influence. (p. 214-215)

21. Explain the causes and effects of learned helplessness. (p. 215-217)

22. Describe the consequences of being placed in a dependent role. (p. 218)

KEY TERMS

anticonformity
autokinetic effect
locus of control
low-ball procedure

coercive power
compliance
conformity
door-in-the-face effect
expert power
foot-in-the-door effect
illusion of control
independence
informational influence
learned helplessness
legitimate power
lure technique
mindfulness
noncontingency
normative influence
obedience
reactance
referent power
reward power
self-categorization
self-induced dependence

COMPLETION ITEMS

Yielding to group pressure when no direct request is made is called (1)______________. There are two basic reasons for conformity. When people are unsure about what is correct, the responses of other people may clarify the situation, thus demonstrating (2)_____________ influence. Conformity based on a desire to be like the others in the group, or to be liked and accepted illustrates (3)______________ influence. The desire to conform to a group may be increased if a person thinks of himself or herself as a member of that group. This reflects the importance of (4)______________-______________. Two reasons have been noted for <u>not</u> conforming. Acting upon one's beliefs regardless of group norms represents (5)______________. Opposing the majority response on all occasions just to be different represents (6)______________.

Conformity increases as the size of the group (7)______________. However, a relatively small group of 3 or 4 can exert a lot of influence if they are all regarded as independent sources of opinion. Conformity increases as the discrepancy between the person and the group (8)______________. The amount of conformity pressure is drastically reduced if the others in the group are not (9)______________ in their opinion.

Yielding to a direct request is called (10)______________. Asking a person to comply with a small request, then making a larger request illustrates the (11)______________-____-____-______________ effect. Compliance with the first request (12)____________ the amount of compliance with the second request. Agreement with the smaller request may result in changes in one's self-perception, as when agreeing to help in a small way on a community problem may cause one to think of himself or herself as a concerned citizen. Agreement with the larger request may be more likely because it is (13)______________ with this (14)______________-______________.

Following the refusal of an extremely large request with a smaller request illustrates the (15)______________-____-____-____________ effect. This procedure (16)______________ compliance with the second request. A technique very similar to the door-in-the-face technique involves a first request followed by an immediate concession. This technique, which resembles late night television advertisements which throw in extra bonuses with a purchase, is called the (17)______________ ____ _____________ technique. The door-in-the-face effect and the that's not all technique occur because the second (smaller) request is seen as a (18)______________, and the person may feel the need to (19)______________.

A car salesperson who gets a customer to agree on a price, then says the manager would not approve the deal and requests a few hundred dollars more is using the (20)______________-______________ procedure. Enticing people to the store to buy a product, then telling them that it is no longer available and trying to sell a substitute product of lesser value illustrates the (21)______________ technique. Both techniques often work because once a person has made a (22)______________, he or she is unlikely to back out.

Compliance to obtain a reward represents (23)______________ power. Compliance with someone who seems to have greater knowledge illustrates (24)______________ power. Compliance to avoid punishment illustrates (25)______________ power. Complying with the requests of a person elected to lead a group represents (26)______________ power. Compliance based on respect, admiration, and wanting to be like a particular person represents (27)______________ power.

Following a direct order from someone in authority such as a government official represents (28)______________. Milgram's shock experiment demonstrated that people can be induced to show very (29)______________ amounts of obedience.

Langer's research suggests that people seem to have an illusion of (30)______________, and tend to (31)______________ their ability to determine the course of events. One of the factors contributing to deterioration of nursing home residents is (32)______________ of (33)______________. The concept of (34)______________ ______________ suggests that people differ in how much personal control they perceive. When our sense of personal freedom is threatened, as when someone tells us we must do something, we are likely to experience psychological (35)______________. In such cases, we may resist the demands.

The belief that one can do nothing to achieve desired outcomes is called (36)______________ ______________. This state leads to a variety of problems such as (37)______________ motivation, reduced learning,(38)______________ depression, and lower self-esteem. When a person who expects to have control is placed in a situation that limits control, their first reaction may be (39)______________, but continued exposure to uncontrollable situations may result in (40)______________ ______________. Placing people in a situation where they are made to feel dependent may reduce subsequent performance, illustrating the process of (41)______________-______________ dependence. Being able to exert control over one's environment seems to increase the person's alertness and awareness, resulting in a state of (42)______________.

COMPLETION ITEM ANSWER KEY

(Answers printed in **bold type** require an exact match, but synonyms are acceptable for other items.)

1. **conformity**
2. **informational**
3. **normative**
4. **self-categorization**
5. **independence**
6. **anticonformity**
7. increases
8. increases
22. **commitment**
23. **reward**
24. **expert**
25. **coercive**
26. **legitimate**
27. **referent**
28. **obedience**
29. great

9. unanimous
10. **compliance**
11. **foot-in-the-door**
12. increases
13. consistent
14. **self-perception**
15. **door-in-the-face**
16. increases
17. **that's not all**
18. **concession**
19. **reciprocate**
20. **low-ball**
21. **lure**
30. **control**
31. overestimate
32. lack
33. **control**
34. **locus of control**
35. **reactance**
36. **learned helplessness**
37. decreased
38. increased
39. **reactance**
40. **learned helplessness**
41. **self-induced**
42. **mindfulness**

MULTIPLE CHOICE ITEMS

1. The Asch conformity study illustrated that:
   a. most people showed complete conformity
   b. people differed greatly in the extent of their conformity
   c. the subjects did not conform
   d. subjects would conform when uncertain, but not when they were confident.

2. In which of the following situations was informational influence the greatest?
   a. Asch's line judging study
   b. Sherif's study of autokinetic effect
   c. studies of the foot-in-the-door effect
   d. demonstrations of anticonformity

3. The extent to which a person conforms to the wishes of a group will be significantly <u>reduced</u> if:
   a. the group is large
   b. the person is insecure
   c. the group is <u>not</u> in complete agreement
   d. the group members independently arrive at the same position.

4. A person who acts differently from everyone else, just to be different illustrates:
   a. conformity
   b. anticonformity
   c. independence
   d. loss of control

5. In situations that involve face-to-face interactions:
   a. women are more likely to conform
   b. men are more likely to conform
   c. men are more likely to yield to normative influence while women are more likely to yield to informational influence
   d. there are no gender differences in conformity

6. Yielding to the direct request of another represents:
   a. conformity
   b. anticonformity
   c. compliance
   d. reactance

7. Dick's boss complains constantly about Dick's beard. Dick is actually tired of the beard, but keeps it just to show that he can do as he pleases. This reflects:
   a. conformity
   b. the low-ball procedure
   c. reactance
   d. self-induced dependence

8. The door-to-door book saleswoman finds that she can sell more books if she first asks people if they will answer a few questions about their reading preferences. This illustrates:
   a. obedience
   b. the low-ball technique
   c. the door-in-the-face technique
   d. the foot-in-the-door technique

9. Nick asks to borrow his dad's car, but before his dad can refuse, he offers to wash it and fill it with gas. This reflects:
   a. the foot-in-the-door technique
   b. the door-in-the-face technique
   c. the low-ball procedure
   d. the "that's not all" technique

10. You agree to drive your friend to the airport. Your friend then informs you that the flight leaves at 6:00 a.m. Your friend used the:
   a. foot-in-the-door technique
   b. door-in-the-face technique
   c. low-ball procedure
   d. reactance principle

11. Your boss asks you to work Thanksgiving day and threatens to fire you if you refuse. This illustrates the use of:
   a. coercive power
   b. reward power
   c. referent power
   d. expert power

12. In the classic Milgram shock study, what percent of the subjects pushed the button to administer the highest shock level (450 volts):
   a. 2%
   b. 25%
   c. 65%
   d. 100%

13. Giving elderly nursing home patients a greater sense of control by letting them care for a plant, arrange the furniture in their room, and voice complaints resulted in:
   a. increased conformity
   b. reactance
   c. self-induced dependence
   d. happier, healthier patients

14. Learned helplessness is greatest if negative outcomes are attributed to:
   a. internal factors
   b. stable factors
   c. global factors
   d. all of the above

15. The foot-in-the-door effect seems to occur because of:
   a. changes in self-perception
   b. needs to reciprocate concessions
   c. needs to establish personal control
   d. referent power

16. In the Asch situation, a subject is asked to make a judgment about:
   a. an ambiguous stimulus
   b. line length
   c. whether to shock another person
   d. whether to exert informational or normative influence

17. Conformity differs from compliance in that in a conformity situation:
   a. no direct request to comply is made
   b. some simple social behavior is involved
   c. there is a direct request or order to do something
   d. most people resist the social influence

18. In the autokinetic effect:
   a. the stimulus is quite clear and unambiguous
   b. a stationary point of light appears to move
   c. not much conformity occurs
   d. college students conform less than others

19. In order for the foot-in-the-door effect to occur:
   a. the initial request must be so small so that the person doesn't even think about the behavior
   b. the person must have the perception of free choice
   c. there must have been external justification for compliance to the initial request
   d. the person must establish an external locus of control

20. In order for the door-in-the-face effect to occur:
   a. the initial request must be small
   b. the subsequent request must be very large
   c. the subsequent request must be made by the same person making the initial request
   d. the request must involve the use of legitimate power

21. Power that is exercised by virtue of superior knowledge is:
   a. coercive power
   b. reward power
   c. expert power
   d. reference power

22. A special form of compliance in which the request is made in the form of an order is:
    a. obedience
    b. conformity
    c. destructive conformity
    d. authoritarianism

23. When events are actually determined by chance, but we believe, nevertheless, that we control them, we are experiencing:
    a. learned helplessness
    b. self-induced dependence
    c. external locus of control
    d. the illusion of control

24. Our belief in control in a chance situation is increased by:
    a. similarity to a real skill situation
    b. lack of involvement in the task
    c. early failure
    d. previous dependency

25. Belief in personal control results in:
    a. good luck
    b. enhanced performance and positive affect
    c. decreased persistence at a task
    d. dissatisfaction with life

26. Responding with greater interest to censored than uncensored material is an example of:
    a. reactance
    b. illusion of control
    c. the door-in-the-face effect
    d. mindlessness

27. Learned helplessness results from experiencing:
    a. control of outcomes
    b. lack of control over outcomes
    c. mindfulness
    d. electric shock

28. Patty saw an ad in the paper offering a free hot air balloon ride to persons who spent the morning picking up litter from the banks of the lake. When she got there she was told that because of high winds, the balloon rides were cancelled, but participants in the litter clean up would get a calendar. She agreed to participate anyway. This scheme to get participants illustrates:
    a. the door-in-the face
    b. the lure
    c. informational influence
    d. mindfulness

MULTIPLE CHOICE ANSWER KEY

1. b	6. c	11. a	16. b	21. c	26. a
2. b	7. c	12. c	17. a	22. a	27. b
3. c	8. d	13. d	18. b	23. d	28. b
4. b	9. d	14. d	19. b	24. a	
5. a	10. c	15. a	20. c	25. b	

SHORT ANSWER ITEMS

1. Distinguish between informational and normative influence, and give an example of each.

2. Distinguish between conformity, compliance, and obedience.

3. Distinguish between the foot-in- the-door technique and the door-in-the-face technique.

4. Why is a sense of control important?

5. When is a loss of control likely to lead to reactance, and when is it likely to lead to learned helplessness?

6. Describe the Milgram studies. What factors influenced the amount of obedience?

APPLICATION QUESTIONS

1. Describe an incident in which you conformed due to informational influence, and an incident in which you conformed due to normative influence.

2. Give a personal example of each of the five bases of power.

3. What do the Milgram studies tell us about social influence?

4. Describe a situation you know about where people have very little control. Describe the consequences of lack of control. What could be done to increase the control of people in that setting?

CHAPTER NINE

AFFILIATION, ATTRACTION, AND LOVE

CHAPTER OUTLINE

Alone or Together

- Loneliness
- Reasons for Affiliation
- Affiliation Patterns and Social Networks

Attraction

- The Basis of Initial Attraction
- Theoretical Models of Attraction

Developing Relationships

- Friendships
- Conceptions and Measurement of Love
- Mate Selection
- Stages in the Development of Love

Falling Out of Love

- Breaking Up Is Hard to Do
- Inequity and Impermanence
- Marriage and Divorce

CHAPTER REVIEW

Loneliness is a subjective experience that results from some deficiencies in a person's social relationships. Emotional loneliness comes from a lack of a close, intimate attachment to someone. Social loneliness involves the lack of people with whom you can interact. Certain events, such as moving to a new community, or a divorce, can result in temporary loneliness which is called state loneliness. People who experience chronic patterns of loneliness suffer from trait loneliness.

We have many reasons for wanting to affiliate with others. Social comparison theory suggests that we sometimes look to others so we can compare and evaluate our attitudes and abilities. We also want to have interactions with other people because they may help reduce anxiety, provide social support, provide interesting company, and for a variety of other reasons.

We are more likely to like people with similar beliefs, values and personalities. We also tend to like those who are physically attractive, like us, and who are in close proximity to us. Reinforcement/affect theory stresses that we like those who reward us. Social exchange theory suggests that relationships depend upon the rewards of both parties. Interdependence theory takes an even more complex view stressing not only the perceived rewards and costs, but also the level of rewards and costs the person has come to expect from relationships (comparison level), and the rewards and costs available in other potential relationships (comparison level for alternatives).

Love is not simply very intense liking. Liking is based on affection and respect, while love involves intimacy, attachment and caring. A variety of types of love or components of love have been described. One common distinction is between passionate love and companionate love. Another approach suggests that love involves intimacy, passion, and commitment. Attachment theory suggest that our early experiences influence the nature of our close relationships. Attachment styles can be secure, we may tend to avoid close relationships, or we may have conflicting feelings both strongly desiring and having much anxiety about close relationships. Equity theory predicts that relationships which are fair to both parties are more permanent.

LEARNING OBJECTIVES

After completing the chapter, you should be able to:

1. Define three characteristics of loneliness. (p. 223)
2. Distinguish between social and emotional loneliness. (p. 223)
3. Distinguish between trait and state loneliness. (p. 224)
4. Explain how attributions and self-presentation strategies influence one's ability to cope with loneliness. (p. 225)
5. Describe some of the reasons why we affiliate with others. (p. 225-227)
6. Explain what is meant by the term social network. (p. 228)
7. Describe 6 factors which are related to liking another person. (p. 229)
8. Explain why proximity frequently leads to liking. (p. 229)
9. Explain when need complementarity seems to be an important determinant of friendship formation. (p. 231-232)
10. Describe three reasons why we might prefer to associate with attractive people. (p. 232-233)
11. List and explain three theories of interpersonal attraction. (p. 233-235)
12. Distinguish between exchange and communal relationships. (p. 234)
13. Distinguish between liking and love. (p. 238-239)
14. Distinguish between passionate and companionate love. (p. 239)

15. Explain the three dimensions of love identified by Sternberg's triangle. (p. 239-240)

16. Describe three attachment styles. (p. 240-241)

17. Describe the general progression of a romantic relationship. (243-244)

18. Explain the importance of equity in the maintenance of a relationship. (247-248)

19. Describe three types of considerations which may be involved in divorce decisions. (p. 248)

KEY TERMS

assortative mating
attachment theory
communal relationship
companionate love
comparison level
comparison level for alternatives
decision/commitment
emotional loneliness
equity theory
ethology
exchange relationship
interdependence theory
intimacy
jealously
loneliness
mere exposure effect
passion
passionate love
propinquity
reciprocal liking
reinforcement/affect theory
social comparison theory
social exchange theory
social loneliness
social network
social support
state loneliness
trait loneliness

COMPLETION ITEMS

Loneliness is not the same as being (1)______________; rather, it is an unpleasant (2)______________ experience that results from some (3)______________ in a person's social relationships. Loneliness caused by the lack of a person to share personal feelings and to have a close, intimate attachment is called (4)______________ ______________. The lack of people to share activities results in (5)_______________ _______________. Temporary loneliness that is caused by situations such as being the only one in your dorm during Spring vacation, or recently breaking up reflects (6)_______________ _______________. Some people show a stable pattern of loneliness called (7)_______________ _______________.

(8)_______________ _______________ _______________ suggests that we often compare our attitudes, skills, or behavior to others in an attempt to evaluate our attitudes and abilities. Interactions with others can cheer us up or help us with stressful situations, thereby providing (9)_______________ _______________. The people with whom we interact regularly compose our (10)_______________ _______________.

We tend to prefer people with (11)_______________ attitudes. We generally prefer people with (12)_______________ personalities, but the theory of need (13)_______________ suggests that some personality differences may fit well together as when a talkative person and a good listener are compatible. We tend to like people who are physically (14)_______________, who do nice things for us, or who have (15)_______________ traits . The concept of (16)_______________ _____________ emphasizes that we usually (17)_______________ a person who likes us. The concept of (18)_______________ emphasizes that most of our friends come from settings in which we are likely to have frequent contact, as when we live near, work with, or sit near another person. The (19)_______________ _______________ effect suggests that we tend to like things that are familiar.

(20)_______________/_______________ theory emphasizes that we tend to like people who reward us. Social (21)_______________ theory notes that it is necessary to consider the rewards and costs of both parties. In casual relationships, people tend to keep track of favors to the other and to keep things in balance; such relationships are called (22)_______________ relationships. Close relationships in which people respond more to the other person's needs than to who "owes" whom are called (23)_______________ relationships. (24)_______________ theory includes the rewards and costs, the person's standard about what level of rewards and costs are fair, and the level of rewards and costs that can be attained elsewhere. The level of rewards and costs that you expect from relationships is termed the (25)______________ ______________. A relationship will be considered satisfactory if the level of rewards and costs that are obtained are more favorable than the (26)______________ ______________. The level of rewards and costs that can be obtained from another relationship is called the (27)_____________ _____________ _____ ______________.

Liking and love seem to be (28)______________ emotions. The, often fleeting, state of intense absorption in another is called (29)______________ ______________. The stable deep affection we feel for a person we love is called (30)______________ love. Love is sometimes said to involve a mixture of three components. A feeling of closeness in the relationship reflects (31)______________. The romantic and sexual aspects of a relationship represent (32)______________. The decision that one is in love and the determination to continue the relationship is called (33)_______________ /______________.

Each individual seems to have a pattern that characterizes his or her close relationships. Three common patterns or(34) ______________ ______________ have been identified. Persons with a (35)______________ attachment style find it fairly easy to develop relationships and are generally comfortable and secure in close relationships. Others, with an (36)______________ attachment style are uncomfortable in close relationships and find it difficult to trust their partner. Persons who want to have a close relationship, but feel very insecure about being close have an (37)______________ /______________ attachment style.

Couples who stay together tend to be more (38)____________ in age, education, intelligence, and attractiveness than couples who break up. Relationships in which the man has a high need for (39)______________ tend to be unstable. (40)______________ theory predicts that relationships that are perceived as fair to both persons are more stable.

COMPLETION ITEM ANSWER KEY

(Answers printed in **bold type** require an exact match, but synonyms are acceptable for other items.)

1. alone
2. subjective
3. deficiencies
4. **emotional loneliness**
5. **social loneliness**
6. **state loneliness**
7. **trait loneliness**
8. **social comparison theory**
9. **social support**
10. **social network**
11. similar
12. similar
13. **complementarity**
14. attractive
15. pleasant
16. **reciprocal liking**
17. like
18. **propinquity**
19. **mere exposure**
20. **reinforcement/affect**
21. **exchange**
22. **exchange**
23. **communal**
24. **interdependence**
25. **comparison level**
26. **comparison level**
27. **comparison level for alternatives**
28. different
29. **passionate love**
30. **companionate**
31. **intimacy**
32. **passion**
33. **decision/commitment**
34. **attachment styles**
35. **secure**
36. **avoidant**
37. **anxious/ambivalent**
38. similar
39. power
40. **equity**

MULTIPLE CHOICE ITEMS

1. A person who frequently feels lonely over a period of several years is probably experiencing:
   a. social loneliness
   b. emotional loneliness
   c. state loneliness
   d. trait loneliness

2. A person who breaks up with their lover, but has a network of friends is likely to experience:
   a. social loneliness
   b. emotional loneliness
   c. trait loneliness
   d. complementary loneliness

3. When Mike learns that his mother is ill, he seeks out his best friend Juan to help him calm down. Juan's comfort and reassurance represents:
   a. social comparison
   b. social support
   c. social evaluation
   d. a social network

4. Social comparison might cause us to seek out other people so we can:
   a. relieve loneliness
   b. reduce anxiety
   c. evaluate our attitudes and abilities
   d. impress others

5. Based on Schacter's experiments on affiliation, you would be unlikely to want to be around other people if:
   a. you were experiencing anxiety
   b. the others were in the same situation as you
   c. the others had no knowledge of your situation
   d. there were few distractions

6. Studies of college students show that:
   a. most people observed on campus are alone
   b. men spend more time interacting with others than do women
   c. most interaction involves people of the same sex
   d. commuter students initially had fewer friends than students living on campus

7. Which of the following truisms is best supported by research on interpersonal attraction?
   a. birds of a feather flock together
   b. absence makes the heart grow fonder
   c. opposites attract
   d. too many cooks spoil the broth

8. For both men and women, physical attractiveness is positively related to:
   a. assertiveness
   b. the amount of social contact with relatives
   c. the amount of social contact with the same sex
   d. the quality of social interactions

9. People are more likely to become friends with those living near them in an apartment complex than with those living farther away. This reflects:
   a. propinquity
   b. reciprocal liking
   c. complementarity
   d. social exchange

10. The level of costs and rewards one expects from relationships reflects the:
    a. payoff level
    b. comparison level
    c. comparison level of alternatives
    d. equity point

11. Rubin found that:
    a. love is simply very intense liking
    b. men love their partner much more than women do
    c. men like their same sex friends more than they like their partner
    d. men show less love for a same sex friend than women show for a same sex friend

12. Whenever Evelyn really cares about a man, she falls head over heels and wants to rush right into a serious relationship. At the same time, she feels very insecure about her partner's love for her. Which of the following describes her attachment style?
    a. secure
    b. avoidant
    c. companionate
    d. anxious/ambivalent

13. Jealousy is likely when a person wants an exclusive relationship and:
    a. is not truly in love
    b. feels inadequate
    c. has a high level of love, but a low level of liking
    d. has a high level of both passionate and companionate love

14. In dating relations, most break ups:
    a. occur because of arguments about sex
    b. occur because of the woman's desire for power
    c. were more likely to be initiated by the woman than by the man
    d. occurred because the man got bored with the relationship

15. Relationships tend to be more stable if:
    a. both partners perceive the relationship to be equitable
    b. there are no barriers to escaping the relationship
    c. the couple dated for at least three years before marriage
    d. the people are high in physical attractiveness

16. When an individual does not have companions that are desired for casual interaction, he or she may experience:
    a. social loneliness
    b. hallucinations
    c. emotional loneliness
    d. social comparison

17. The lonely college student and the contented college student are most clearly distinguished by the presence of:
    a. romantic partners
    b. friends
    c. dates
    d. pets

18. Compared to women, men:
    a. are less likely to discuss their personal feelings with same-gender friends
    b. see their friends more frequently
    c. are more likely to end a relationship
    d. fall in love more slowly

19. Studies of the relationship between attitude similarity and attraction find that the two are related:
    a. only in the artificial environment of the laboratory
    b. in both the lab and the field
    c. negatively
    d. only among college students

20. Need complementarity:
    a. probably operates on only a few dimensions and in a limited number of situations
    b. explains why "birds of a feather flock together"
    c. is a pervasive finding in studies of new acquaintances
    d. is more important for women than for men

21. Dion (1972) found that, compared to those who are less attractive, physically attractive children are:
    a. given harsher punishments for misbehavior
    b. treated less like adults
    c. treated more leniently
    d. more intelligent

22. The positive effects of physical attractiveness of a date seem to be transferable:
    a. from a woman to a man
    b. from a man to a woman
    c. neither (a) nor (b)
    d. both (a) and (b)

23. In women, physical attractiveness is associated with:
    a. greater assertiveness
    b. greater likelihood of initiating contacts with men
    c. less intelligence
    d. less developed social skills

24. The mere exposure effect probably accounts for the effects of _____ on attraction.
    a. physical attractiveness
    b. competence
    c. reciprocal liking
    d. propinquity

25. The basic principle of the reinforcement-affect theory of interpersonal attraction is that:
    a. we like people who reward us and dislike people who punish us
    b. we strive to maintain a balance between our own net outcomes from a relationship and those of our partner
    c. we maintain those relationships in which the rewards we receive are greater than those of our partner
    d. we try to maximize the number of affective relationships in which we're involved

26. An important way in which social exchange theory differs from reinforcement-affect theory is that social exchange theory:
    a. focuses on the rewards a person may gain from a relationship
    b. considers both rewards and punishments
    c. considers both people involved in a relationship
    d. is concerned with the outcomes of alternative relationships

27. Divorce is more likely for people who:
    a. marry young
    b. have low achievement needs
    c. have little ambition
    d. all of the above

MULTIPLE CHOICE ANSWER KEY

1. d	6. c	11. d	16. a	21. c	26. c
2. b	7. a	12. d	17. b	22. a	27. a
3. b	8. d	13. b	18. a	23. d	
4. c	9. a	14. c	19. b	24. d	
5. c	10. b	15. a	20. a	25. a	

SHORT ANSWER ITEMS

1. Describe at least six factors that might lead to interpersonal attraction.

2. List at least six of the rules that Argyle & Henderson identified as central to friendship.

3. Describe Rubin's model of loving and liking.

4. How does jealousy seem to differ for men and women?

5. Describe at least four factors which are related to the stability of romantic relationships and/ or marriages.

APPLICATION QUESTIONS

1. Describe a time when you were lonely. Was it an example of trait or state loneliness? Social or emotional loneliness?

2. Think of a close friend. Describe how the factors listed as likely to lead to friendship apply to this friendship.

3. Use the concepts of interdependence theory to analyze a particular close relationship or a friendship.

4. Characterize your attachment style using one or a combination of the styles described by Hazan & Shaver.

CHAPTER TEN

AGGRESSION AND VIOLENCE

CHAPTER OUTLINE

Aggression and Human Nature

- Definitions of Aggression
- Biological Explanations of Aggression
- Social Explanations of Aggression
- Biology and Learning

Conditions That Influence Aggression

- Frustration
- Aggressive Cues: The Weapons Effect
- General Arousal
- Verbal and Physical Attack
- Third-Party Instigation
- Deindividuation
- Drugs
- Environmental Conditions
- The Role of Anger in Aggression
- Individual Differences in Aggressive Behavior

Violence and the Mass Media

- Television Violence and Aggression in Children
- Pornography and Aggression toward Women

Violence in Society

- Violence in the Home
- Violence in the Streets
- Collective Violence

How Can Aggression Be Controlled?

CHAPTER REVIEW

Aggression involves behavior intended to harm another person or living being. Some theorists take a biological perspective and feel that aggression is an inevitable part of human nature. However, others think aggression is a result of social processes including: learning, socialization, and norms.

Psychoanalysts, ethologists, and sociobiologists emphasize human nature as a cause of aggression. Freud believed that aggression was instinctual and that aggression could be discharged in socially acceptable ways such as a debate or athletics, or in less desirable ways through behavior designed to hurt someone. Ethology and sociobiology emphasize that aggression is a natural occurrence and may have some beneficial effects for the individual or the species.

Aggressive behavior may be learned through instrumental learning and observational learning. Some suggest that instincts and genetics play no part at all in aggression. Regardless of whether this is correct, aggressive tendencies are greatly influenced by learning and other conditions encountered by the individual.

Many factors influence aggression. The frustration-aggression hypothesis emphasizes that frustrations may often stimulate aggression. Aggression is especially likely when a person is angry and is exposed to aggressive cues. The excitation transfer theory suggests that, under certain circumstances, aggression may be increased by various types of arousal. Verbal and physical attacks, instigation by others, feelings of deindividuation, alcohol, and unpleasant environmental conditions may intensify aggression.

Anger is an emotion which plays an important role in some aggression behavior. However, it is important to distinguish between feelings of anger and aggressive behavior. The cognitive-neoassociationistic model suggests that anger and aggression influence each other, but that they are not identical concepts, and one does not completely cause the other. The model suggests the following sequence: An aversive event, such as someone spilling coffee on you, will cause negative emotions. These emotions will trigger both feelings of anger and a desire to behave aggressively.

Certain thoughts are triggered by anger. The nature of the thoughts depend on the person's previous experiences. Depending on the nature of these thoughts, they can increase or decrease the chances of aggressive behavior.

Media portrayal of violence can increase aggression, although several factors may determine how much influence the media violence exerts. Pornography is erotic material which combines aggression and forced sexual behavior. Pornography may result in more aggression toward women, and more acceptance of violence toward women.

Violence is common in the home, as street crime, and in collective violence that occurs in groups. Aggression may be controlled by: channeling aggression into socially desirable behaviors, limiting cues that trigger aggression, observation of nonaggressive models, nonreinforcement of aggression, the use of effective punishment procedures, triggering incompatible responses such as humor or empathy, limiting frustrations, and by providing information about mitigating circumstances.

LEARNING OBJECTIVES

After completing Chapter 10, you should be able to:

1. Define aggression. (p. 254)

2. Contrast the biological and social explanations of aggression. (p. 255-259)

3. Describe the operation of two types of learning which may lead to aggressive behavior. (p. 258)

4. Explain at least three factors which might influence the extent of aggression follows frustration. (p. 259-261)

4. Describe the effect of aggressive cues. (p. 261-262)

5. Describe excitation transfer theory. (p. 262)

6. Describe how people react to physical and verbal attacks. (p. 262-263)

7. Describe the ways how an active or inactive observer can affect aggressive behavior. (p. 264-265)

8. Explain the concept of deindividuation, and tell how it affects aggression. (p. 265-266)

9. Explain the effects of alcohol and marijuana on aggression, and explain the role of provocation on these effects.
(p. 266-267)

10. Describe the effects of noise, air quality, and temperature on aggression, and explain the role of provocation on these effects. (p. 267-268)

11. Describe the cognitive-neoassociationistic model and use it to explain the role of anger in aggression.
(p. 268-270)

12. Describe three ways in which very aggressive people differ from others in the processing of social information.
(p. 270-271)

13. Explain the basic effect of media violence on aggressive behavior and discuss observational learning and cognitive explanations for the effect. (p. 271-274)

14. Define pornography, and explain its effects on aggression, and related attitudes. (p. 274-276)

15. Discuss the frequency of violence in the United States.
(p. 276-277)

16. Describe the concept of relative deprivation and explain its role in collective violence. (p. 278-279)

17. Describe the prospects for controlling aggression and the basic approach advocated by those with a biological view of aggression. (p. 279)

18. Describe four possible ways of controlling aggression that reflect social or cultural views of aggression. (p. 279-281)

KEY TERMS

aggression
aggressive cue
catharsis
cognitive-neoassociationistic model
collective violence
deindividuation
egoistic deprivation
ethology
excitation transfer theory
fraternal deprivation
frustration
frustration-aggression hypothesis
fundamental attribution bias
instrumental learning
instrumental value
modeling
neo-Freudians
observational learning
pornography
releaser
scripts
sociobiology
third-party instigation

COMPLETION ITEMS

Aggression is (1)_______________ intended to harm or injure another (2)_______________ _______________. Aggression includes both physical harm and (3)_______________ aggression such as insults. Freud and other psychoanalysts, believed that we have aggressive (4)_______________. According to them, if these instinctual urges are not expressed indirectly in socially appropriate activities, they will result in (5)_______________. The subfield of biology that is concerned with instincts common to all members of a species is called (6)_______________. Ethologists such as Konrad Lorenz believe that, across the animal kingdom, aggression serves many (7)_______________ purposes, but for humans causes problems because we have not learned to inhibit our aggression. The systematic study of the biological basis of social behavior is called (8)_______________.

Aggression may lead to reinforcements such as social approval or getting what we want; thus, aggression may be learned through (9)_______________ _______________. In addition, we often acquire aggressive behavior by watching other people, thus demonstrating (10)______________ ______________. Observing aggression may tell us that aggression is appropriate. Observational learning is also called (11)______________.

The (12)______________-______________ ______________ states that aggression is a result of frustration. However, the link between frustration and aggression is not automatic. In addition to aggression, a variety of other reactions may be caused by (13)______________. Furthermore, several factors such as the arbitrariness of the frustration and the presence of aggressive cues may determine whether frustration leads to (14)______________. Weapons or other stimuli associated with violence may serve as (15)______________ ______________ and (16)______________ the amount of aggression. The (17)______________ ______________ theory suggests that arousal from other sources can increase aggression. Aggression is very likely following a verbal or physical (18)______________.

Aggression can be (19)______________ by the presence of a person who encourages or seems to approve of the aggression. In conditions where personal identity is not stressed, persons may experience (20)______________ and be (21)______________ likely to express aggression when angry. Large amounts of alcohol may (22)______________ aggression, but only when the person is (23)______________. Marijuana seems to (24)______________ aggression. When a person has been provoked, unpleasant stimuli such as loud noise or hot temperatures may (25)______________ aggression.

Berkowitz has developed a model to explain how aversive events can result in anger and aggression. This model is called the (26)______________-______________ model. It suggests that anger can influence aggressive behavior, but is not the major cause of (27)______________. Aversive events trigger (28)______________ affect, a state of general dislike. Negative affect produces both instigations to (29)______________ and feelings of(30)______________. Because anger may prime thoughts about aggressive behaviors, anger can influence whether the person behaves (31)______________.

Some people are generally more aggressive than others. These differences may result from differences in how people process social information. Aggressive people tend to attribute more (32)______________ intent to the actions of others. Aggressive people seem to be more likely to think of aggressive responses and to have more (33)_______________ attitudes about engaging in aggressive behavior.

Both laboratory and field studies indicate that media violence tends to (34)_______________ aggression. This effect may be explained in terms of (35)_______________ learning and also in cognitive terms since media may serve as a priming device making aggression more (36)_______________ in memory. Frequent exposure to media violence may also desensitize a person to aggression. The link between media violence and aggressive behavior may depend on many factors such as whether the violence is justified, whether the viewer (37)_______________ with the violent model, whether the violence is thought to be real, and whether others condemn the violence.

Erotic material that combines explicit sexual content, sexual coercion, and aggression is called (38)_______________. Exposure to such material sometimes leads to (39)_______________ aggression directed toward (40)_______________, but no change in aggression toward (41)_______________.

About (42)______% of married couples have engaged in physical violence toward a spouse. The United States has the (43)_______________ crime rate of all industrialized nations. Collective violence, such as riots, is more likely when people experience (44)_______________ _______________.

A variety of suggestions have been offered to control aggression. Instinct theorist suggest channeling (45)_______________ into socially acceptable behaviors. A (46)_______________ model can decrease aggression. Under appropriate conditions, punishment for aggression can be effective. In addition, nonreinforcement of aggressive responses may (47)_______________ aggression. The concept of (48)_______________ suggests that if you let off steam and get your anger out, you will be (49)_______________ likely to act aggressively in the immediate future. While expressing aggression at the time of a frustration does reduce later aggression, behavioral catharsis does (50)_______________ reduce the overall incidence of aggression.

COMPLETION ITEM ANSWER KEY

(Answers printed in **bold type** require an exact match, but synonyms are acceptable for other items.)

1. behavior
2. living being
3. verbal
4. **instincts**
5. **aggression**
6. **ethology**
7. positive
8. **sociobiology**
9. **instrumental learning**
10. **observational learning**
11. **modeling**
12. **frustration-aggression hypothesis**
13. **frustration**
14. **aggression**
15. **aggressive cues**
16. increase
17. **excitation transfer**
18. **attack**
19. instigated
20. **deindividuation**
21. more
22. increase
23. provoked
24. decrease
25. increase
26. **cognitive-neoassociationistic**
27. **aggression**
28. **negative**
29. **aggression**
30. **anger**
31. **aggressively**
32. hostile
33. favorable
34. increase
35. observational
36. accessible
37. identifies
38. **pornography**
39. increased
40. women
41. men
42. **25**
43. highest
44. **relative deprivation**
45. aggression
46. nonaggressive
47. decrease
48. **catharsis**
49. less
50. not

MULTIPLE CHOICE ITEMS

1. Which of the following is <u>not</u> an example of aggression?
   a. Mary Ann gets mad at her husband and yells obscenities at him
   b. Jeannette's car won't start so she kicks in the door
   c. Mack is mad at his girlfriend and, in anger, kicks his dog
   d. Len tries to hit Bob, but misses

2. The existence of nonaggressive societies is cited as evidence for which type of theory of aggression?
   a. Freudian
   b. neo-Freudian
   c. ethological
   d. learning

3. In order to build his own status, Bill insults Keith and tries to make him look foolish in a meeting. This represents aggression based on:
   a. instrumental learning
   b. observational learning
   c. deindividuation
   d. frustration

4. Sally is a new supervisor at work and sees another supervisor yell at employees. Sally concludes that yelling at employees is acceptable behavior and starts to yell at her employees. Sally's aggression was increased by:
   a. observational learning
   b. sociobiology
   c. instrumental learning
   d. frustration

5. Frustration is <u>less</u> likely to lead to aggression if:
   a. the frustration is severe
   b. aggression has instrumental value
   c. the frustration causes anger
   d. the frustration was accidental rather than arbitrary

6. Aggressive cues:
   a. increase the chances that an angry person will express aggression
   b. decrease the chances that an angry person will express aggression
   c. lead to frustration
   d. relieve frustration

7. Which of the following persons would exhibit the most aggression?
   a. a person who had been frustrated
   b. a person who had three mixed drinks and watched a film of an exciting track meet
   c. a person who had been insulted by a boxer and then watched a boxing film
   d. a person who had been relieved of all aggressive cues

8. The excitation transfer theory suggests that:
   a. aggression may be increased by types of arousal other than anger
   b. frustration rarely leads to aggression
   c. aggression leads to the preservation of the species
   d. insults always lead to aggression

9. The presence of others will:
   a. increase aggression
   b. decrease aggression
   c. have no effect on aggression
   d. increase aggression only if the other persons are thought to approve of aggression

10. Increased aggression when people feel anonymous results from:
    a. excitation transfer
    b. deindividuation
    c. catharsis
    d. sociobiological factors

11. How does the use of alcohol and marijuana affect a person's response to provocation?
    a. Large amounts of alcohol or marijuana increase aggression
    b. Large amounts of alcohol or marijuana decrease aggression
    c. Large amounts of alcohol increase aggression while large amounts of marijuana decrease aggression
    d. Large amounts of alcohol decrease aggression while large amounts of marijuana increase aggression.

12. Unpleasant noise levels:
    a. increase aggression regardless of provocation
    b. increase aggression if a person is provoked
    c. reduce the impact of frustration
    d. cause men to be more aggressive and women to become less aggressive

13. The number of murders and rapes:
    a. have decreased dramatically in the last 10 years
    b. are greater in hot weather
    c. are closely related to changes in the stock market
    d. are lower in the United States than in Europe

14. Most of the studies of television and media violence suggest that:
    a. media violence causes aggression
    b. media violence serves as a safety valve and prevents aggression
    c. media violence does not influence aggression
    d. only combinations of sex and violence increase aggression

15. Televised violence is <u>less</u> likely to lead to aggressive behavior if:
    a. the child hears an adult condemn the violence
    b. the child identifies with the violent character
    c. the child thinks the violence is real
    d. the child watches a great deal of television violence

16. Angry men who watch a pornographic film:
    a. are less aggressive because they are sexually aroused
    b. are more aggressive toward both men and women
    c. are more aggressive toward men and less aggressive toward women
    d. are more aggressive toward women, but not toward men

17. An American Indian who feels that Indians are getting much less than they deserve in terms of jobs, education, and government assistance feels:
    a. fraternal deprivation
    b. maternal deprivation
    c. egoistic deprivation
    d. ethological deprivation

18. According to Lorenz, human aggression is worse than animal aggression because we:
    a. have failed to evolve inhibitory mechanisms
    b. kill for food
    c. have natural tendencies to be aggressive
    d. have a stronger instinct

19. Which of the following see(s) aggression as instinctual or biologically based?
    a. ethology
    b. psychoanalytic theory
    c. sociobiology
    d. all of the above

20. Berkowitz' cognitive-neoassociationistic model proposes that aversive events such as frustration or attack produce:
    a. inhibition of aggression
    b. negative affect
    c. deindividuation
    d. avoidance of aggressive cues

21. The lower homicide rate in countries, such as Canada, with strict control over firearms, is consistent with laboratory findings of a(n):
    a. modeling effect
    b. excitation transfer effect
    c. deindividuation effect
    d. weapons effect

22. Bandura's Bobo doll experiments demonstrated that children:
    a. will be more aggressive when they have attractive toys to play with
    b. will model adult aggressive behavior
    c. are more aggressive than adults
    d. have instinctual drives for aggression

23. Aggression may be decreased by:
    a. high temperatures
    b. loud noise
    c. a nonaggressive model
    d. an instigation to aggression

24. Societies characterized by very little aggression tend to:
    a. exist in fairly inaccessible places not coveted by others
    b. be oriented toward more abstract, less concrete, aspects of life
    c. have highly differentiated sex roles
    d. be highly materialistic

25. Television violence is most common in:
    a. prime-time programming
    b. children's cartoons
    c. daytime drama
    d. comedy shows

26. Field research has demonstrated that knowing how much television children watch at age 8 tells us about:
    a. how aggressive they will be at age 18
    b. how they will respond to pornography
    c. how aggressive their parents are
    d. how aggressive they were at age 4

27. Collective violence is most likely to occur when:
    a. objective conditions reach an all-time low
    b. people experience relative deprivation
    c. religious ties are weakened
    d. confidence is bolstered by rising outcomes

28. Punishment may be a deterrent to aggression if:
    a. it is not predictable
    b. it follows the aggressive behavior immediately
    c. the persons administering it are seen as aggressive models
    d. the punishment must violate existing social norms

29. Individuals with a history of violence are more likely than others to:
    a. have a "hostile attribution bias"
    b. have difficulty thinking of nonaggressive responses
    c. feel more positive about aggressive behaviors
    d. all of the above

30. According to the cognitive-neoassociationistic model, anger:
    a. develops only as an after-the-fact justification of aggressive behavior
    b. always leads to aggression
    c. sometimes leads to increased aggression
    d. never leads to increased aggression

MULTIPLE CHOICE ANSWER KEY

1. b	6. a	11. c	16. d	21. d	26. a
2. d	7. c	12. b	17. a	22. b	27. b
3. a	8. a	13. b	18. a	23. c	28. b
4. a	9. d	14. a	19. d	24. a	29. d
5. d	10. b	15. a	20. b	25. b	30. c

SHORT ANSWER ITEMS

1. Contrast biological and social explanations of aggression.

2. Describe eight factors that influence aggression.

3. What factors influence the amount of aggression that follows frustration?

4. Describe the cognitive-neoassociationistic model. Use it to explain the relationship between anger and aggression.

5. Describe the effects of media violence on aggression. What factors affect this effect. Use both observational learning and cognitive concepts to explain why media violence can lead to increased aggression.

6. Under what circumstances does viewing pornography lead to increased aggression and related attitudes?

7. Describe at four ways in which aggression can be reduced.

APPLICATION QUESTIONS

1. Describe how instrumental learning and observational learning may have influenced your aggressive tendencies.

2. Think of an instance where you displayed either verbal or physical aggression. Which of the conditions that influence aggression listed in the text relate to your behavior?

3. If you were a parent, what could you do to keep your children from becoming highly aggressive?

CHAPTER ELEVEN

PROSOCIAL BEHAVIOR

CHAPTER OUTLINE

Are We Capable of Truly Altruistic Behavior?

- Traditional Psychological Theories and Altruism
- The Empathy-Altruism Hypothesis
- Challenging the Empathy-Altruism Hypothesis
- Biology, Culture, and Altruism

A Decision-Making Model of Helping

Situational Influences of Prosocial Behavior

- The Person in Need of Help
- The Influence of Other Bystanders

Personal Influences of Prosocial Behavior

- Searching for the Good Samaritan
- Moods and Helping

Seeking and Receiving Help: The Recipient's Perspective

Toward a Prosocial Society

- Raising Prosocial Children
- Encouraging Adults to Give

CHAPTER REVIEW

Prosocial behavior is behavior (such as cooperation, sharing or giving aid) that benefits others or has positive social consequences. Helping behavior is prosocial behavior that benefits others more than oneself. Altruism is helping behavior that is selfless and is motivated only by desires to help others. Altruistic behavior is designed to relieve someone's suffering or to make things better for the person. Altruism does not include helping that is designed to reduce guilt, gain social approval, or make the helper feel good about himself or herself. Helping motivated by such concerns is called egoism and is based on self-interest rather than altruism.

Becoming aware of someone's need can result in two different emotional reactions: empathic concern and personal distress. Empathic concern involves feeling sympathy or compassion for the person and being concerned that the person is relieved of the suffering. The empathy-altruism hypothesis suggests that feelings of empathy can lead to truly altruistic behavior. Feelings of personal distress involve being worried, alarmed, or disturbed by the plight of another person. These feelings often lead to helping behavior. However, since such helping is designed to improve the helper's emotional state, it is not selfless, but egoistic and does not meet the definition of altruism. The negative-state relief model suggests that what appears to be altruism may really be egoistic. The model suggests that we experience sadness or other negative emotions when we see someone in distress. Helping makes us feel better, resulting in relief from the negative emotional state.

Because altruism does not benefit the person giving help, traditional theories have difficulty accounting for altruism, and have developed a variety of ways of accounting for seemingly altruistic behaviors. Biologically and genetically based theories have developed concepts such as kin selection and reciprocal altruism to explain the origin of altruism. These concepts suggest that even though altruism does not insure the survival of the helper, altruism may have evolved because it is good for the species. Other theorists suggest that altruistic motives may be learned from one's culture through the operation of cultural values and social norms.

The arousal/cost-reward model suggests that helping can be thought of as a decision-making process which involves both cognitive and emotional elements. Helping requires: noticing the need, becoming emotionally aroused, interpreting the arousal as indicating concern for the victim's welfare, evaluating rewards and costs of both helping and failing to help, and taking action.

A variety of situational factors exert strong influences on helping. People are more likely to receive aid if they: have a legitimate need, the need is not the person's fault, the person is someone the helper knows, the person is pleasant or similar to the helper. Feelings of ambivalence may cause people to be inconsistent in their willingness to help a person of another race or a disabled person.

The presence of unresponsive bystanders greatly reduces helping, but if others show alarm or take action, they often increase helping. Through social influence, unresponsive bystanders may cause a person to interpret a situation as a nonemergency. Through audience inhibition, a person may not offer help because he or she thinks that bystanders would not approve or the helping behavior. When other bystanders are in a position to help, diffusion or responsibility may occur, making each person less likely to help.

Some personality and background factors (such as a highly developed sense of morality, and a sense of competence to help) have been shown to predict helping, but the relationships are often weak and fairly inconsistent. Moods, and the accompanying thoughts, also influence the extent of helping. Helping is more likely when a person is in a good mood and focused on his or her good fortune. Feeling guilty or being concerned for the misfortunes of others may lead to more helping, but being preoccupied with one's own problems inhibits helping.

Receiving help may threaten self-esteem of the recipient. Help is more likely to be welcomed if it does not threaten the recipient's self-esteem. Help may lead to greater self-reliance and independence or to dependence depending upon the recipient's sense of control.

Children are generally egoistic, but can learn to be more concerned for others. These changes seem to result form increased empathy that comes from maturity and from learning norms of prosocial behavior.

LEARNING OBJECTIVES

After completing Chapter 11, you should be able to:

1. Distinguish between altruism and helping behavior. (p. 286)

2. Distinguish between altruism and egoism. (p. 286)

3. Describe the empathy-arousal hypothesis. (p. 288)

4. Distinguish between empathic concern and personal distress. (p. 288)

5. Describe the negative-state relief model. (p. 290)

6. Describe a biologically based explanation of prosocial behavior. (p. 291-293)

7. Describe how culture and learning might lead to prosocial behavior. (p. 293-294)

8. Distinguish between collectivist and individualist cultures, and explain how they may affect prosocial behavior. (p. 293)

9. Describe the social responsibility norm, and the reciprocity norm, and give an example of when each might lead to prosocial behavior. (p. 293)

10. Describe the 5 basic steps in the arousal/cost-reward model. (p. 294-296)

11. Explain, and give examples of what is meant by the costs of helping, and costs of not helping. Explain how both factors influence one's response to a person in need. (p. 295)

12. Describe one important limitation of the arousal/cost-reward model. (p. 295-296)

13. Explain how the clarity, legitimacy, and controllability of a person's need affect helping. (p. 296)

14. Describe how at least three characteristics of the person in need affect helping. (p. 297-298)

15. Describe the bystander effect, and describe three processes which cause it. (p. 298-300)

16. Describe the urban-overload hypothesis and explain how it can affect helping behavior. (p. 300)

17. Describe at least three factors which tend to distinguish helpers from non-helpers. (p. 300-304)

18. Describe how mood affects helping. (p. 304-305)

19. Explain how the level of self-esteem and sense of control of the person receiving help can affect his or her reaction to help. (p. 305-308)

20. Describe how and why children and adults differ in altruism. (p. 308-309)

KEY TERMS

altruism
arousal/cost-reward model
audience inhibition
bystander effect
collectivist culture
costs of helping
costs of not helping
diffusion of responsibility
egoism
empathic concern
empathy
empathy-altruism hypothesis
helping behavior
individualistic culture
kin selection
negative-state relief model
personal distress
personal norms
prosocial behavior
psychoanalytic theory
reciprocal altruism
reciprocity norm
self-monitoring
social influence
social-responsibility norm
sociobiology
urban-overload hypothesis

COMPLETION ITEMS

Behavior that benefits others or has positive social consequences is called (1)_____________ _____________. A subset of prosocial behavior that clearly benefits others rather than the self is called (2)_____________ _____________. Completely selfless behavior motivated only by desires to help others reflects (3)_____________. There is much debate about the nature of helping behavior; some psychologists even doubt whether (4)_____________ exists. Helping may lead to subtle rewards such as increased self-esteem, or relief from negative emotions, and thus not be truly altruistic, but rather reflect (5)_____________ or self-interest.

Being truly moved and able to feel genuine sympathy for the suffering of another represents the experience of (6)_____________. The theory that predicts that empathy can result in altruistic behavior is called the (7)_____________-_____________ _____________. Another reaction to the suffering of others is to feel personally upset, disturbed, or worried. This egoistic feeling of uneasiness is called (8)_____________ _____________. It contrasts with (9)_____________ _____________ which reflects concern for the other person's suffering. Thus, a person who sees a bleeding accident victim and feels sympathy experiences (10)_____________ _____________, while a person who experiences feelings of revulsion at the sight of the blood feels (11)_____________ _____________. Persons are most likely to help, even though they could escape the distressing situation, if they are experiencing (12)_____________ _____________. Some theorists believe that even if a person has empathy, their helping may not be totally altruistic. Concern for the suffering of another person may produce negative emotions such as sadness. The (13)_____________ _____________ _____________ _____________ suggests that helping someone in need may simply be a means to improve the helper's mood.

From the evolutionary perspective of sociobiology, altruism might promote (14)_____________ _____________, the survival of the kinship group's genes. The concept of (15)_____________ _____________ suggests that genes that foster altruism would be useful in the long run because altruistic acts would be reciprocated. Cultural norms and values can also promote altruism. Cultures which stress the best interests of the group over individual desires are called (16)______________ cultures. Cultures which place less emphasis on personal responsibility for the welfare of others represent (17)______________ cultures. Prosocial behavior is stressed more in (18)______________ ______________. Cultural norms provide standards for behavior, including helping behavior. Thinking that we should help those in need reflects the (19)______________-______________ ______________. Feeling the need to help one who has helped us reflects the (20)______________ ______________.

Helping may be thought of as a decision-making process in which both cognitive and emotional processes influence decisions to help. A prominent decision-making model, Piliavin's (21)______________ / ______________-______________ model, suggests that helping requires five steps: becoming aware that help is needed, experiencing emotional (22)_____________, (23)_________________ the arousal as concern for the person's welfare, analysis of (24)______________ and (25)______________ of helping, and finally, taking action. Factors such as effort or time involved in helping, and possible danger or embarrassment represent (26)_____________ _____ ______________. Guilt, loss of self-esteem, and a knowledge that the person continues to suffer are (27)______________ _____ _______ _____________. Increases in self-esteem, recognition, and living
up to personal norms may represents (28)______________ for helping.

We are (29)______________ likely to help a person who is truly dependent, especially if the dependency occurred through no (30)________________ of the person. We are generally more likely to help relatives, friends and acquaintances than to help (31)______________. We are more likely to help someone who is pleasant, attractive, or (32)______________ to ourself. Many people may have ambivalent feelings about handicapped persons and members of other races, thus leading to (33)______________ tendencies to help such people.

People are less likely to help if (34)______________ bystanders are present, illustrating the (35)______________ ______________. This effect occurs because of three processes: a (36)______________ ______________ process (responses of bystanders influence the person's interpretation of the situation), (37)______________ ______________ (where the person worries about what others will think), and (38)______________ ______ ______________ (where the person doesn't think it is his or her job to help). Responsive bystanders can (39)______________ helping through the process of (40)____________.

The (41)______________-______________ ______________ suggests that because so many people are encountered each day, city people must be selective in who they help. People in good moods because of their own good fortune are (42)______________ likely to help. The (43)______________-______________ ______________ ______________ suggests that helping can be one way of overcoming a bad mood. Bad moods caused by empathic sadness for a friend may (44)______________ helping, while sadness about one's personal problems will not.

Receiving help may lead to negative reactions if it threatens the (45)______________-______________ of the recipient. Children are generally (46)______________ altruistic than adults. However, as children gain maturity, they become better able to take the perspective of others and experience (47)______________. As a child grows, he or she may learn norms that support helping, observe adult models, and gain experience at behaving in helpful ways. These experiences can (48)______________ a child's prosocial behavior.

COMPLETION ITEM ANSWER KEY

(Answers in **bold type** require an exact match, but synonyms are acceptable for other items.)

1. **prosocial behavior**
2. **helping behavior**
3. **altruism**
4. **altruism**
5. **egoism**
6. **empathy**
7. **empathy-altruism hypothesis**
8. **personal distress**
9. **empathic concern**
10. **empathic concern**

26. **costs of helping**
27. **costs of not helping**
28. **rewards**
29. more
30. fault
31. strangers
32. similar
33. inconsistent
34. unresponsive
35. **bystander effect**
36. **social influence**

11. **personal distress**
12. **empathic concern**
13. **negative state relief model**
14. **kin selection**
15. **reciprocal altruism**
16. **collectivist**
17. **individualist**
18. **collectivist**
19. **social-responsibility norm**
20. **reciprocity norm**
21. **arousal/cost-reward**
22. **arousal**
23. labeling
24. rewards
25. costs
37. **audience inhibition** (or **evaluation apprehension**)
38. **diffusion of responsibility**
39. increase
40. **modeling**
41. **urban-overload hypothesis**
42. more
43. **negative-state relief model**
44. increase
45. **self-esteem**
46. less
47. **empathy**
48. increase

MULTIPLE CHOICE ITEMS

1. Behavior that benefits another person and that was motivated solely by a desire to help the other person is defined as:
   a. altruism
   b. egoism
   c. helping behavior
   d. prosocial behavior

2. Which of the following suggests that helping can be motivated by purely unselfish motives?
   a. the arousal/cost-reward model
   b. the empathy-altruism hypothesis
   c. the negative states relief theory
   d. the diffusion of responsibility theory

3. The arousal/cost-reward model suggests that:
   a. altruism is inherited
   b. altruism is taught by society
   c. helping is a decision-making process
   d. helping is impulsive

4. In which situation is the person <u>least</u> likely to help?
   a. The person is experiencing personal distress and the situation is easy to escape
   b. The person is experiencing personal distress and the situation is difficult to escape
   c. The person is experiencing empathic concern and the situation is easy to escape
   d. the person is experiencing empathic concern and the situation is difficult to escape

5. A friend's parent dies and you feel sympathy, compassion, and feel for your friend's grief. Your response represents:
   a. personal distress
   b. egoism
   c. negative states relief
   d. empathic concern

6. We are especially likely to offer help:
   a. to people who need help because of reasons beyond their control
   b. to members of minority groups
   c. to strangers
   d. if other bystanders are unresponsive

7. Ambivalent feelings toward racial minorities and the handicapped leads to:
   a. more helping
   b. less helping
   c. inconsistent levels of helping
   d. high degrees of empathy

8. The bystander effect suggests that:
   a. people willingly stand by and watch others provide help
   b. people are more likely to help if bystanders are present
   c. individuals are less likely to help if unresponsive bystanders are present
   d. bystanders often band together to provide help

9. Concern that if you try to help you will make a fool of yourself illustrates:
   a. social influence process
   b. audience inhibition
   c. diffusion of responsibility
   d. personal norms

10. Joe is in a theater when the manager announces a bomb threat. A very superficial inspection of the theater fails to reveal a bomb, so the movie starts again. Joe sees that the others in the audience don't look terribly concerned. He concludes the bomb threat is a hoax and continues to watch the movie. His lack of concern is probably a result of:
    a. social influence
    b. audience inhibition
    c. diffusion of responsibility
    d. personal norms

11. Observing a person giving aid tends to:
    a. create empathy for the person receiving help
    b. increase the chances that others will also give aid
    c. decrease the chances that others will give aid
    d. not affect the tendency of others to give aid

12. In a series of studies that support the negative state relief model, even subjects who were feeling empathy were less likely to provide help if:
    a. they were given a surprise cash gift
    b. they expected to hear a comedy tape
    c. they thought their mood had been stabilized by a drug
    d. all of the above

13. Being in a good mood because you made an A on your chemistry test tends to:
    a. increase helping
    b. decrease helping
    c. increase helping only if the person receiving the help is physically attractive
    d. decrease helping of strangers, but increase helping of friends

14. Being in a bad mood will:
    a. increase helping
    b. decrease helping
    c. increase helping if the person is concerned about others
    d. increase helping if the person is concerned about themselves

15. Persons who need help:
   a. will always appreciate the help
   b. may resent help if it threatens their self-esteem
   c. always resent the help
   d. will invariably become more dependent as a result of receiving help

16. Prosocial behavior:
   a. always involves a great cost to the helper
   b. is always based on unselfish motives
   c. has positive social consequences
   d. can easily be explained by major psychological theories

17. Psychoanalytic theory assumes that human nature is basically:
   a. selfish
   b. selfless
   c. altruistic
   d. learned

18. Caroline is at a concert and sees a man fall on a step and hit his head. He gets up, staggers to a seat, and rests his head in his hands. According to the arousal/cost-reward model, in order for Caroline to help the man, she must:
   a. believe that the man needs help
   b. determine that helping the man is worth her effort
   c. feel emotional arousal that she believes was a result of the injury
   d. all of the above

19. Sociobiologists explain altruism as adaptive from an evolutionary perspective because it:
   a. increases the probability of the survival of the species' genes
   b. enhances the survival of the fittest individuals
   c. makes clear our relationship to lower animals
   d. aids in reproduction

20. The arousal/cost-reward model of helping suggests that:
    a. cognitive factors play little part in responses to emergencies
    b. because the required responses have to happen so quickly, there is clearly an instinctive basis to our behavior in emergencies
    c. awareness of a person in need can produce arousal which may motivate helping
    d. we fail to consider rewards and costs of helping

21. Asking one of the many people sitting near you at the ball game to watch your things while you go to the rest room is an attempt to counteract:
    a. diffusion of responsibility
    b. negative states relief
    c. audience inhibition
    d. egoism

22. Cognitive distortion that incorrectly convinces a person that a situation is not an emergency and doesn't require help is most likely when:
    a. the person has altruistic motives
    b. the person is in a good mood
    c. the costs of helping and the costs of not helping are both high
    d. all of the above

23. The reciprocity norm says that we should help those who:
    a. are in need of help
    b. are deserving of help
    c. have helped us
    d. are related to us

24. People are more likely to receive help when their need is:
    a. under their control
    b their own fault
    c. great
    d. small

25. The study comparing the helping behavior of high and low self-monitors suggested that:
    a. high self-monitors help more
    b. high self-monitors help less
    c. high self-monitors help more only if social norms encourage helping
    d. high self-monitors have more empathy

26. The negative state relief model proposes that prosocial behavior:
    a. usually has some costs associated with it
    b. may result in more positive feelings
    c. is based on altruistic motives
    d. often makes a bad mood worse

27. Help is most likely to lead to independent behavior such as getting off welfare when:
    a. it does not threaten the recipient's self-esteem
    b. it is based on altruistic motives
    c. it is based on egoistic motives
    d. the recipient maintains a sense of control of his or her life

MULTIPLE CHOICE ANSWER KEY

1. a	6. a	11. b	16. c	21. a	26. b
2. b	7. c	12. d	17. a	22. c	27. d
3. c	8. c	13. a	18. d	23. c	
4. a	9. b	14. c	19. a	24. c	
5. d	10. a	15. b	20. c	25. c	

SHORT ANSWER ITEMS

1. Why is it difficult to develop a theoretical explanation for altruism?

2. Distinguish between altruism and egoism. Why is it difficult to demonstrate that helping is motivated by purely altruistic concerns?

3. Describe the five steps in the arousal/cost-reward model of helping.

4. How is emotional arousal related to helping?

5. How are norms related to helping?

6. How are moods and thoughts related to helping?

APPLICATION QUESTIONS

1. Think of an incident in which you were aware that someone might need help. How do the steps of the arousal/ cost-reward model relate to your decision-making in that incident?

2. Think of a situation in which you helped someone and an incident in which you decided not to offer help. How did your feelings and situational influences differ in these two cases?

3. Think of a time when you helped someone. To what extent was your helping motivated by altruistic concerns and by egoistic concerns?

CHAPTER TWELVE

BEHAVIOR IN GROUPS

CHAPTER OUTLINE

The Influence of Other People

- The Effects of an Audience
- The Effects of Coactors
- The Effects of Other Group Members

Group Composition and Structure

- Group Size
- Communication Networks
- Leadership
- Roles and Expectations

Interaction in Groups

- Problem Solving
- The Perils of Groupthink
- The Polarizing Effects of Group Interaction
- Minority Group Influence

Group Socialization

- Basic Processes
- Stages of Group Socialization
- The Influence of Culture

CHAPTER REVIEW

People who are around one another but do not interact or influence one another represent an aggregate. A group is two or more people who have interactions with one another. Groups can vary in many ways including the amount and types of interaction, the degree of influence, the extent of commitment, and permanence.

The presence of others will have greater social impact if there are many others, they are closer, and of high status. The presence of others watching a person perform will cause increased performance (social facilitation) on simple or well learned tasks, but hurt performance if the task is difficult or poorly learned (social inhibition). These effects may be due to arousal, expected evaluations, or distractions caused by the presence of others. Performance in the presence of others who are working (coactors) may also be influenced by social comparison when a person compares his or her performance to the performance of others.

Group structure represents regular patterns of interactions between members such as roles, norms, and status. The ideal size for a group seems to depend upon factors such as the nature of the group task, the group structure, and whether member satisfaction or efficiency is most important. Communication networks represent the patterns of communications between persons in the group; they influence the leadership, morale and performance of the group. Various roles or functions develop in groups. Norms are expectations about appropriate behavior of group members. Status characteristics theory deals with the development of status hierarchies in groups such that some members are more highly regarded than others.

Two major dimensions of leadership exist: consideration and initiating structure. Contingency models of leadership suggest that the best approach to leadership depends upon the situation. Fiedler's contingency model categorizes leaders according to their evaluations of their least preferred co-worker. Low LPC leaders (who rate their least preferred co-worker negatively) are motivated by successful performance, while high LPC leaders are motivated to achieve good interpersonal relations. Low LPC leaders are appropriate in situations where the leader has either very much or very little control, while high LPC leaders are appropriate for situations with moderate control.

Social loafing refers to a tendency of members to slack off on a task. This effect may reflect motivational losses and coordination problems. Groups may be better than an individual at solving problems, but the nature of the task and the nature of the individuals can greatly influence group effectiveness. Groupthink represents a problem that occurs when a group's striving for concurrence overrides rational decision making, and as a result, the group makes a poor decision. Group polarization indicates that, as a result of group discussion, group members' opinions may become more extreme.

Group socialization refers to the changes that occur as a person becomes involved in a group, participates in the group, and leaves the group. This process involves stages of investigation, socialization, maintenance, resocialization, and remembrance, along with various role transitions. These stages reflect varying evaluations of the group and the member and varying degrees of commitment.

LEARNING OBJECTIVES

After completing Chapter 12, you should be able to:

1. Distinguish between an aggregate and a group. (p. 314)

2. Describe social impact theory and the three factors which determine the amount of impact. (p. 315)

3. Describe social facilitation and social impairment effects and explain when each is likely to occur. (p. 315-317)

4. Discuss the arousal-drive model of audience effects. (p. 317-318)

5. Explain the distraction-conflict theory of social facilitation and social impairment. (p. 318-319)

6. Describe social loafing and explain why it occurs, and explain four things that can reduce it. (p. 321)

7. Explain what is meant by group structure. (p. 322)

8. Describe how communication networks can affect leadership, satisfaction, and performance in a group. (p. 324-325)

9. Describe two major clusters of leader behaviors. (p. 325-326)

10. Explain what is meant by a contingency model of leadership. (p. 326)

11. Describe the four basic components of Fiedler's contingency model. (p. 326-327)

12. Describe the leadership styles of high LPC and low LPC leaders and indicate when each type is likely to be effective. (p. 326-328)

13. Distinguish between specific and diffuse status characteristics, and explain how they contribute to status distinctions in groups. (p. 329)

14. Explain groupthink, and describe the basic symptoms. (322-323)

15. Describe five antecedents of groupthink. (p. 322-323)

16. Describe three procedures for avoiding groupthink. (p. 334)

17. Describe group polarization and give two reasons why it occurs. (p. 334-336)

18. Explain how persons with a minority viewpoint can influence the majority. (p. 336-338)

19. Describe three basic processes that are important to group socialization. (p. 338-339)

20. Describe two stages and two transitions that must occur before a person is accepted as a full member of a group.

21. Describe the possible reactions of a group and a member when they begin to diverge. (p. 342-343)

KEY TERMS

aggregate
arousal-drive model
autokinetic effect
brainstorming
leader position power
LPC
mind guard
minority influence

coactor
cohesiveness
communication network
consideration
contingency model
deindividuation
diffuse status characteristic
distraction conflict theory
fundamental attribution bias
group
group polarization
group socialization
group structure
groupthink
immediacy
informational influence
initiating structure
leader/member relations
normative influence
norms
number
production blocking
risky shift
role
role differentiation
role expectations
social comparison
social facilitation
social impact theory
social inhibition
social loafing
specific status characteristic
status characteristics theory
strength
task structure
uncertainty of approval

COMPLETION ITEMS

A collection of individuals who do not interact with one another is called an (1)______________. Two or more people who do interact are called a (2)______________. The influence of an audience is described in Latane's (3)______________ ______________ theory. This model predicts (4)______________ impact if the audience is large. Whether the audience is physically close reflects (5)______________, while the status of the audience might reflect its (6)______________.

When an audience results in improved performance, this reflects (7)______________ ______________. When the presence of others hurts performance, (8)______________ ______________ has occurred. Zajonc explained these results by suggesting that an audience produces (9)______________ which leads to an increased tendency to produce (10)______________ responses. An explanation of social facilitation and impairment that is based on attentional conflict is called the (11)______________-______________ theory. A person working near others who are working on the same type of task is in the presence of (12)______________. Seeing how our performance stacks up against the performance of other people illustrates (13)______________ ______________. When people are working in groups, they may slack off reflecting (14)______________ ______________.

The term (15)______________ ______________ represents the regular pattern of relationships between group members. It includes such things as systems of roles, norms, and status. Prescribed patterns of communication are called (16)______________ ______________. A central person in a communication network is likely to have (17)______________ control than people in peripheral positions. Networks with decentralized communication tend to have (18)______________ morale than networks with limited communication opportunities.

Attempts to classify leadership behaviors resulted in two major clusters of behaviors. Warmth, trust, and open communication represent the cluster called (19)______________. The other cluster, (20)______________ ______________ emphasizes the development of well-defined procedures, goals, and patterns of organization. Leadership models that suggest that there is no all-purpose, best style of leadership, but that the effectiveness of any style depends on the circumstances are called (21)______________ models. Fiedler's contingency model suggests that the most important situational factor is (22)______________/ ______________ ______________. When the leader can do things like determine pay rates, and fire people, the situation is high in (23)______________ ______________ ______________. If the goals and appropriate work methods are clear, then the situation is high in (24)______________ ______________. In situations with very high or very low situational control, a (25)______________ LPC leader is most effective. In situations with moderate amounts of situational control, a (26)______________ LPC leader is best.

Group members may occupy various positions or (27)______________. People occupying certain positions are expected to act in certain ways, reflecting the (28)______________ ______________. These positions often evolve in the course of group interaction, illustrating the process of (29)______________ ______________. Behaviors expected of all group members, such as being nice to other members or following required procedures, are called (30)_______________. Most groups develop status hierarchies. The (31)_______________ _______________ theory explains some of the factors on which status distinctions are based.

A group problem solving approach which encourages members to express any and all ideas and delays evaluation of ideas is called (32)_______________. When groups show so much concurrence seeking that they fail to realistically evaluate their decisions, they are exhibiting (33)_______________. This problem is especially likely to occur in groups that are close knit or highly (34)_______________, but where the members are (35)_______________ of approval from the group, and have a highly (36)_______________ leader.

The concept of (37)_______________ _______________ suggests that when groups reach consensus, the judgments and opinions may become more (38)_______________ than they were before the group participation. Changing one's position just to be in agreement with other group members reflects the (39)_______________ influence explanation of group polarization. The (40)_______________ _______________ explanation says that polarization occurs because people are persuaded by the content of the arguments presented in the group discussion. While the majority usually exerts more influence, at times persons in the (41)_______________ can exert substantial influence.

Becoming a part of a group involves moving through five stages of group (42)_______________. Both the prospective member and the group check each other out during the (43)_______________ stage. If the person and the group hit it off, the person reaches the role transition of (44)_______________ and becomes a new member of the group and begins the (45)_______________ stage where the a process of mutual adjustment begins. If the person and the group are able to fit well together, the person passes from new member to member, marking the role transition of (46)_______________. The stage at which a person is functioning as a full member of the group is called (47)_______________. If the relationship becomes strained, the role transition of (48)_______________ marks the beginning of the (49)_______________ stage. Unless the person and the group can successfully find a way to fit together, the role transition of (50)______________ is followed by the (51)______________ stage.

COMPLETION ITEM ANSWER KEY

(Answers printed in **bold type** require an exact match, but synonyms are acceptable for other items.)

1. **aggregate**
2. **group**
3. **social impact**
4. greater
5. **immediacy**
6. **strength**
7. **social facilitation**
8. **social inhibition**
9. **arousal**
10. **dominant**
11. **distraction-conflict**
12. **coactors**
13. **social comparison**
14. **social loafing**
15. **group structure**
16. **communication network**
17. greater
18. higher
19. **consideration**
20. **initiating structure**
21. **contingency**
22. **leader/member relations**
23. **leader position power**
24. **task structure**
25. low
26. high
27. **roles**
28. **role expectations**
29. **role differentiation**
30. **norms**
31. **status characteristics**
32. **brainstorming**
33. **groupthink**
34. **cohesive**
35. uncertain
36. directive
37. **group polarization**
38. extreme
39. **normative**
40. **informational influence**
41. minority
42. **socialization**
43. **investigation**
44. **entry**
45. **socialization**
46. **acceptance**
47. **maintenance**
48. **divergence**
49. **resocialization**
50. **exit**
51. **remembrance**

MULTIPLE CHOICE ITEMS

1. The impact of an audience is greater if:
   a. there are only a few people in the audience
   b. the audience is of high status
   c. the audience is some distance away
   d. the task is well learned

2. When a person performs a difficult task for the first time, an audience is likely to:
   a. improve performance
   b. hurt performance
   c. have no affect on performance
   d. calm the person

3. Anna is learning to type. She does pretty well, but when the teacher comes by to observe she makes errors. This illustrates:
   a. social comparison
   b. social facilitation
   c. social inhibition
   d. the modeling effect

4. Kim likes to do impersonations of the president. When her friends ask her to perform for a group, her imitation is even better than usual. This improved performance illustrates:
   a. social comparison
   b. social facilitation
   c. social inhibition
   d. the modeling effect

5. Less arousal occurs in the presence of a blindfolded audience than an audience that is able to see. This suggests that an important reason behind social facilitation and inhibition is:
   a. concern over being evaluated
   b. innate drives
   c. social comparison
   d. competition

6. Each evening Stephanie goes to an aerobics class. The others in the class represent:
   a. an audience
   b. coactors
   c. a dominant response group
   d. an aggregate

7. The best size for a group is:
   a. as small as possible
   b. as large as possible
   c. eight to ten people
   d. variable, depending upon the task and the amount of structure

8. In which of the following networks do personalities and skills of the members have the most impact in determining which members are dominant?
   a. wheel
   b. chain
   c. Y
   d. circle

9. Which of the following communication networks leads to the best performance?
   a. a wheel
   b. a circle
   c. a wheel is best for simple tasks and a circle is best for complex tasks
   d. a wheel is best for complex tasks and a circle is best for simple tasks

10. A leader who determines appropriate work procedures, assigns tasks to particular members, and generally keeps the group focused on their goal shows:
   a. consideration
   b. initiating structure
   c. high-LPC leadership
   d. contingent leadership

11. A leader who: treats members with respect, mutual trust, and warmth shows:
   a. consideration
   b. initiating structure
   c. low-LPC leadership
   d. contingent leadership

12. According to Fiedler, which of the following is the <u>most</u> important factor in determining the favorability of a situation for leadership?
    a. leader/member relations
    b. task structure
    c. goal clarity
    d. position power

13. Fiedler's contingency theory of leadership points out:
    a. that some individuals have the traits necessary to be an effective leader in any situation.
    b. that leader characteristics are really irrelevant; the effectiveness of a leader depends entirely on the situation
    c. that certain kinds of leaders function best in certain kinds of situations; that is, leader characteristics interact with situational characteristics
    d. permissive leaders never function very well in real-life groups

14. High LPC leaders are most effective in situations that are:
    a. very unfavorable
    b. very favorable
    c. moderately favorable or unfavorable
    d. extremely favorable or unfavorable

15. All members of a particular campus organization are expected to maintain a B average. This reflects a:
    a. norm
    b. role
    c. role expectation
    d. status characteristic

16. A person's status in a group is determined by:
    a. specific status characteristics
    b. diffuse status characteristics
    c. both specific and diffuse status characteristics
    d. group dynamogenesis

17. On a basketball team, a person's ability to rebound represents:
    a. a specific status characteristic
    b. a diffuse status characteristic
    c. an aggregate characteristic
    d. a cohesiveness factor

18. Glenn and Bobby often fish together for bass. After a while a pattern develops where Bobby uses large lures for largemouth bass and Glenn uses small lures for smallmouth bass. This represents:
    a. status characteristics
    b. social facilitation
    c. brainstorming
    d. role differentiation

19. Barry works for a large mowing crew that cuts the grass on a college campus. Because the supervisor only knows how much the entire crew mows, Barry realizes he can take it easy and takes frequent rest breaks. This represents:
    a. social facilitation
    b. social inhibition
    c. social loafing
    d. groupthink

20. Groupthink occurs because:
    a. members aren't concerned about the group's decision
    b. members are too concerned with keeping the group in agreement
    c. the group has too much conflict
    d. the leader fails to take charge

21. Which of the following leads to group polarization?
    a. group members fail to take the task seriously
    b. most persuasive arguments support the group's initial leaning
    c. groups tend to be very cautious
    d. women have much less influence than men in most groups

22. A minority is often more successful at convincing the majority if they appear to be:
    a. consistent
    b. disinterested
    c. unfair
    d. weak

23. A collection of individuals who do not interact with one another is a(n):
    a. aggregate
    b. group
    c. collective
    d. cohesion

24. According to research on social loafing, decreased effort may take place in a group setting <u>unless</u>:
    a. the overall task is boring
    b. the group is large
    c. the performance of each individual can be identified
    d. the person thinks others are loafing

25. A group problem solving technique (in which all members are encouraged to express whatever solutions come to mind with no evaluations until everyone's ideas have been expressed) is:
    a. brainstorming
    b. group comprehension
    c. the random thought procedure
    d. mind averaging

26. Janis proposed that groupthink is most likely to develop in groups that:
    a. are highly cohesive
    b. consult with qualified outsiders
    c. have a leader that encourages critical thinking
    d. are too small

27. The "risky shift" is an example of:
    a. groupthink
    b. brainstorming
    c. group polarization
    d. social facilitation

28. Explaining group polarization by suggesting that individuals in a group shift their opinions in order to be in closer agreement with the opinion of the group characterizes the:
    a. brainstorming explanation
    b. normative influence explanation
    c. informational influence explanation
    d. groupthink explanation

29. In Moreland and Levine's (1982) model of group socialization, the process by which members (or potential members) assess the rewards that the group provides is known as:
    a. role transition
    b. commitment
    c. evaluation
    d. divergence

30. When a group member gets mad at the rest of the group and looses some of his or her interest in the group, the person's membership in the group is in the:
    a. maintenance stage
    b. resocialization stage
    c. exit stage
    d. remembrance stage

MULTIPLE CHOICE ANSWER KEY

1. b	6. b	11. a	16. c	21. b	26. a
2. b	7. d	12. a	17. a	22. a	27. c
3. c	8. d	13. c	18. d	23. a	28. b
4. b	9. c	14. c	19. c	24. c	29. c
5. a	10. b	15. a	20. b	25. a	30. b

SHORT ANSWER ITEMS

1. What factors determine the amount of social impact exerted by an audience?

2. When are social facilitation and social inhibition likely to occur? Discuss the various theories that account for social facilitation and inhibition effects.

3. How are communication networks related to morale, control, and group performance?

4. List and describe the two basic dimensions of leader behavior.

5. Describe Fiedler's contingency model. What does the name mean? What are the three factors that determine the favorability of a leadership situation. What type of leader is most appropriate for an extremely favorable, moderately favorable, and highly unfavorable leadership situation.

6. Describe the causes and symptoms of groupthink.

7. Describe group polarization and give two explanations.

APPLICATION QUESTIONS

1. Describe a time when you experienced social facilitation and a time when you experienced social inhibition. Using concepts discussed in this chapter explain why your performance improved in one situation and deteriorated in another.

2. Think of a group to which you belong or have belonged. Describe the structure of that group.

3. Describe a time when you engaged in social loafing.

4. Think of a leader that you know, and estimate his or her levels of consideration and initiating structure. How do these factors affect your feelings about the leader and your willingness to follow his or her directions?

5. Think of a group to which you belong, and classify the leadership situation according to Fiedler's contingency model. What type of leader is most appropriate for this situation? What style does your leader show? How effective is your leader?

6. Think of a group to which you belong or have belonged. Describe how the model of group socialization applies to your involvement in this group.

CHAPTER THIRTEEN

BEHAVIOR BETWEEN GROUPS

CHAPTER OUTLINE

Similarities and Differences among Groups

- The Social-Psychological Tradition
- Overlapping Distributions
- Questions of Causality

Cross Cultural Comparisons

- Universal of Culture-Specific?
- Some Research Examples

Prejudice and Discrimination

- Racism
- Sexism
- Causes of Prejudice and Discrimination

In-Groups and Out-Groups

- Categorization and Social Identity
- Views of the In-Group and Out-Group

Strategies of Interaction

- Cooperation and Competition
- Bargaining and Negotiation
- Third-Party Intervention

Reduction of Intergroup Conflict

- Superordinate Goals
- Intergroup Contact
- Reduction of Threat

CHAPTER REVIEW

This chapter examines a number of issues related to group membership. First, it examines the extent to which principles of social psychology are general across various cultures and across gender and race. Then, it focuses on how group membership affects thoughts and interactions of individuals. Finally, it examines conflict and ways of reducing conflict between groups and individuals.

Differences between groups may reveal general patterns, but group differences do not mean that all people within each group reflect the patterns. Even when groups differ in terms of some characteristic, all individual members do not show this pattern. For example, the average man is taller than the average woman, but we can easily think of short men and tall women. It is often difficult to explain the cause of differences between groups because the groups may differ in a variety of hereditary and environmental factors that cannot be readily separated for analysis.

Cross-cultural psychology attempts to understand the similarities and differences in behavior across cultures. Etic constructs concern factors that are universal across cultures, while emic constructs are culture specific. Factors such as emotional display rules, degree of acceptance of various groups, and emphasis on individualism have been shown to vary across cultures.

Intergroup behavior involves interaction between members of different groups when the interaction is somehow based on their group identifications. Prejudice involves intolerant, unfair, or unfavorable attitudes toward a group of people. Discrimination refers to unfair behavior directed toward a group. Stereotypes are beliefs about the characteristics of a certain category of people such as a racial, occupational, or grender group. Racism includes both racial prejudice and discrimination by an individual or institution. Sexism involves gender-based prejudice and discrimination. A number of causes for prejudice and discrimination have been identified.

We seem to have a strong tendency to classify people as part of a group to which we belong (in-group) or as an outsider (out-group). Ethnocentrism reflects a tendency to see one's own group more positively than other groups.

A cooperative reward structure occurs when everybody "sinks or swims" together. A competitive reward structure occurs when success by one party makes success more difficult or impossible for the other party. Competitive reward structures foster intergroup rivalry by: inhibiting open communication, distorting perceptions, and encouraging the use of force.

Procedures for reducing conflict include: bargaining, third-party intervention, superordinate goals, intergroup contact (under appropriate conditions), and the GRIT strategy of reduction of threat.

LEARNING OBJECTIVES

After completing Chapter 13, you should be able to:

1. Define intergroup behavior. (p. 348)

2. Explain how the concept of overlapping distributions relates to comparisons between groups. (p. 349-350)

3. Explain the difficulty in determining causes of group differences. (p. 350-352)

4. Describe both the purpose of and need for cross-cultural psychology. (p. 352-355)

5. Distinguish between etic and emic constructs and give an example of each. (p. 352-355)

6. Distinguish between prejudice, discrimination, and stereotypes. (p. 355)

7. Use the concepts of spontaneous processes and controlled processes to explain the major difference between prejudiced and unprejudiced people. (p. 355-356)

8. Describe how racism has changed in the last few decades. (p. 356-359)

9. Discuss the importance of belief similarity and race. (p. 358-359)

10. Define racism and sexism. (p. 356-359)

11. Describe the typical stereotypes of men and women, and explain why they are not equally favorable. (p. 359-360)

12. Describe six types of explanations for the existence of prejudice. (p. 362-364)

13. Explain the meaning of in-groups and out-groups and give an example which illustrates each. (p. 364)

14. Describe social categorization and explain how it affects judgments of others. (p. 364-370)

15. Define ethnocentrism and give an example. (p. 367-369)

16. Distinguish between cooperative, competitive, and individualistic reward structures. (p. 371)

17. Describe the jigsaw method and its major effects. (p. 371-372)

18. Describe three ways in which a competitive situation can affect interpersonal relations. (p. 372-373)

19. Distinguish between a compromise and an integrative agreement. (p. 375-376)

20. Explain how the presence of a third party may affect the resolution of conflict. (p. 376)

21. Define a superordinate goal, give an example, and explain how a superordinate goal can affect conflict resolution. (p. 377)

22. Describe the conditions that must be met before intergroup contact is likely to reduce conflict. (p. 377-378)

23. Describe the basic process of the GRIT approach. (p. 378-379)

KEY TERMS

arbitration
bargaining
belief-similarity hypothesis
competition
competitive reward structure
cooperation
cooperative reward structure
cross-cultural psychology
cultural script
discrimination
display rules
emic constructs
ethnocentrism
etic constructs
exotic bias
gender-role norm
GRIT
individualistic reward structure
in-group
integrative agreement
intergroup behavior
intergroup contact hypothesis
jigsaw method
mediation
modern racism
out-group
prejudice
racism
scapegoating
sexism
social distance
stereotype
superordinate goal
symbolic racism
ultimate attribution bias

COMPLETION ITEMS

Attempts to determine the generality of basic psychological principles across various societies or cultural groups is the goal of (1)______________-______________ psychology. While differences may exist between different cultural or racial groups or between people of different genders, the distributions of behavior show much (2)______________. Because personal and environmental factors are so highly intertwined, it is difficult to establish the exact (3)______________ of cross-cultural differences. For example, differences in the behavior of women and men may have a physiological basis, or may reflect beliefs about appropriate behavior of men and women. These beliefs are called (4)______________-______________ ______________.

Concepts which are universal and apply to all cultures represent (5)______________ ______________, while culture specific concepts are called (6)______________ ______________. Problems arise when (7)______________

______________ are thought to apply to all cultures. A (8)______________ ______________ is a pattern of social interaction that is typical of a particular cultural group. For example, the Hispanic script of simpatica suggests that people are generally friendly and likable.

(9)______________ ______________ occurs when people from one group interact with people from another group and the actions are influenced by the stance or values of the groups. Intolerant, unfair attitudes and negative feelings toward some group of people reflect (10)______________. Unfair behavior toward members of that group reflect (11)______________. Beliefs about the characteristics of members of an identifiable group represent (12)______________. One model of prejudice distinguishes between spontaneous and controlled processes. The activation of stereotypes seems to be (13)______________ and occur in both prejudiced and (14)______________ persons. The primary difference between prejudiced and unprejudiced persons is that unprejudiced persons (15)______________ the negative beliefs contained in the stereotype and avoid the prejudiced response.

Racial prejudice, discrimination, or discriminatory institutional structure is called (16)______________. Racism can occur at either the individual or (17)______________ level, as when a company's or a country's policy is unfair to some racial group. While blatant racism may be less socially accepted than in the past, sometimes racist attitudes may be expressed in attitudes on issues relevant to ethnic groups (i.e., affirmative action, a holiday honoring Martin Luther King). Such, less obvious, forms of racism are called (18)______________ ______________ or modern racism.

Discrimination and prejudice based on gender is called (19)______________. According to the prevelant stereotype, men are thought to be competent and independent while women are thought to be (20)______________ and expressive. Because of such stereotypes, successful performance of (21)______________ is more likely to be attributed to luck while successful performance of a (22)______________ is usually attributed to ability.

Gordon Allport described several levels of explanation of prejudice and discrimination. Based on the historical and economic perspective, Karl Marx suggested that

(23)______________ might be used by the "haves" to justify exploitation of the "have nots". Displacement of hostility to less powerful groups is called (24)______________. The (25)______________ emphasis suggests that prejudice results from the way we perceive the world. Suggestions that stereotypes of people who have extensive contact with a group have a "kernel of truth" illustrates an emphasis on an (26)______________ ______________.

We seem to have a stong tendency to categorize people. The most basic categorization is in terms of a group to which we belong called an (27)______________-______________. A persons not in our group is an (28)______________-______________ member. We tend to accentuate differences between groups, but to (29)______________ differences among members of the same out-group. Using one's own group as a standard to see how other groups measure up, and thinking of one's group as superior illustrates (30)______________. This can lead to biased explanations of the successes and failures of in-groups and out-groups. According to the (31)______________ ______________ ______________, attributions to in-group members successes are likely to stress stable internal causes, while we are likely to use situational causes to explain the success of out-group members.

When the situation is such that one individual (or group) can attain the reward only if the other person (or group) also attains the reward, then a (32)______________ ______________ ______________ exists. A situation in which one person or group attaining a reward decreases the opportunity for the other person or group to reach a reward, is a (33)______________ ______________ ______________. When a person's chances of reaching the goal is not influenced by whether another person or group reaches their goal, then an (34)______________ ______________ ______________ exists. One example of creating a cooperative reward structure to increase interracial cooperation in a school setting is the (35)______________ ______________. (36)______________ reward structures foster intergroup rivalry, decrease effective communication, cause distorted (37)______________, and often result in the use of force. Most conflicts between groups are mixed-motive situations because they involve elements of both (38)______________ and competition.

The process of give and take, where parties try to settle a dispute, is called (39)______________. When both parties concede to a middle ground, a (40)______________ solution has been reached. If the parties can find a solution that results in high payoffs for all concerned, then an (41)______________ ______________ has been reached. At times, it is useful to have a third-party work to help conflicting parties reach a settlement. When the third-party plays only an advisory role, the process is called (42)______________. If the third-party can impose a solution on the other parties, then the process is called (43)______________.

In the Robber's Cave study, conflict was reduced through a series of (44)______________ ______________. The idea that interaction will reduce conflict is proposed in the (45)______________ ______________ ______________. However, it seems that several conditions must occur before intergroup contact is likely to reduce conflict. The (46)______________ model is a strategy to decrease conflict whereby one party starts to gradually reduce threat.

COMPLETION ITEM ANSWER KEY

1. **cross-cultural**
2. overlap
3. causes
4. **gender-role norms**
5. **etic constructs**
6. **emic constructs**
7. **emic constructs**
8. **cultural script**
9. **intergroup behavior**
10. **prejudice**
11. **discrimination**
12. **stereotypes**
13. spontaneous
14. unprejudiced
15. inhibit
16. **racism**
17. institutional
18. **symbolic racism**
19. **sexism**
20. warm
27. **in-group**
28. **out-group**
29. minimize
30. **ethnocentrism**
31. **ultimate attribution bias**
32. **cooperative reward structure**
33. **competitive reward structure**
34. **individualistic reward structure**
35. **jigsaw method**
36. **competitive**
37. **perceptions**
38. **cooperation**
39. **bargaining**
40. **compromise**
41. **integrative agreement**
42. **mediation**

21. woman
22. man
23. **prejudice**
24. **scapegoating**
25. **phenomenological**
26. **earned reputation**

43. **arbitration**
44. **superordinate goals**
45. **intergroup contact hypothesis**
46. **GRIT**

MULTIPLE CHOICE

1. Traditional social psychology tends to emphasize:
   a. cross-cultural psychology
   b. situational factors
   c. genetic factors
   d. personality differences

2. When comparing our society to another society, we tend to:
   a. focus on similarities between the two societies
   b. display great admiration for the other culture
   c. show an exotic bias
   d. focus on how the other society is better than our own society

3. Social distance refers to:
   a. how closely people stand when interacting
   b. the degree to which we are willing to engage in various forms of social interaction with a member of an identifiable group
   c. the degree of dissimilarity between two cultures
   d. the amount of information that is available about another culture

4. Which of the following seems to be the most culturally universal:
   a. spontaneous expression of emotion
   b. display rules
   c. reliance on the equity norm
   d. the expectation that others are generally likable and fun to be with

5. Some cross-cultural theorists have proposed that some economically-oriented models of social behavior developed in the U.S., like equity theory, may apply:
   a. very broadly across all cultures
   b. to friendly behavior but not to unfriendly behavior
   c. to interactions with members of the same gender, but not to members of the opposite gender
   d. only to people living under capitalism

6. Constructs which are universal and apply to all cultures are called:
   a. emic constructs
   b. etic constructs
   c. ethnocentric constructs
   d. GRIT constructs

7. A waitress who dislikes blacks, but treats all customers well regardless of race shows:
   a. prejudice
   b. discrimination
   c. a cross-cultural perspective
   d. scapegoating

8. Racially prejudiced persons seem to differ from nonprejudiced persons in terms of:
   a. their knowledge of racial stereotypes
   b. the degree of positive and negative thoughts about racial groups
   c. spontaneous activation of racial beliefs
   d. all of the above

9. According to traditional stereotypes, women are more likely than men to be thought to be:
   a. muscular
   b. competitive
   c. warm and expressive
   d. a financial provider

10. Broverman's study of mental health clinicians suggests that the description of a healthy adult person was:
   a. similar to the description of a healthy adult female
   b. similar to the description of a healthy adult male
   c. similar to the description of either a healthy male or female
   d. similar to the description of a healthy child

11. Americans are more likely to believe that:
    a. blacks are discriminated against
    b. women are discriminated against
    c. women are given more preferential treatment than blacks
    d. there is complete equality for both blacks and women

12. The suggestion that prejudice is caused by competition for scarce jobs, or by changes in contemporary family roles illustrates the:
    a. historical and economic emphasis
    b. earned reputation emphasis
    c. psychodynamic emphasis
    d. sociocultural emphasis

13. Results of studies of perceptions of a groups suggests that:
    a. stereotypes are completely inaccurate
    b. stereotypes are extremely accurate
    c. when based on firsthand knowledge, stereotypes may have a kernel of truth
    d. stereotypes displace hostility; therefore, reduce discrimination

14. We are likely to:
    a. see our group as diverse, but see an out-group as homogeneous
    b. see both our group and an out-group as homogeneous
    c. fail to notice differences between the in-group and the out-group
    d. glorify the out-group and fail to appreciate the in-group

15. Members of ten different fraternities and sororities want to convince the university to build a road at the edge of campus so they can all move to a convenient location. In this case, the reward structure for these organizations is:
    a. altruistic
    b. independent
    c. competitive
    d. cooperative

16. Competitive reward structures tend to promote:
    a. effective communication
    b. accurate perceptions of the other group
    c. superordinate goals
    d. the use of force

17. The jigsaw method produced better intergroup relations by creating:
    a. new stereotypes
    b. a cooperative reward structure
    c. a competitive reward structure
    d. an individualistic reward structure

18. Compared to a person bargaining for only oneself, a person who is bargaining for his or her group is:
    a. more likely to reach a quick settlement
    b. more cooperative
    c. less likely to reach agreement
    d. less stubborn

19. Reaching a settlement where all parties are pleased because they get what they hoped for represents:
    a. mediation
    b. arbitration
    c. a compromise
    d. an integrative agreement

20. In Sherif's Robber's Cave study, fixing the broken water line represented:
    a. a superordinate goal
    b. negotiation
    c. a competitive reward structure
    d. a problem that could be solved using the GRIT model

21. When a conflict is solved through mediation:
    a. it is likely to resurface within a matter of days
    b. it is likely to spread to other issues
    c. a third-party is not needed
    d. the parties are usually satisfied with the results

22. Contact between members of conflicting groups is more likely to reduce antagonism:
    a. if status differences are large and are clear to both parties
    b. only if the conflict is very strong
    c. if the persons live up to the negative traits thought to characterize them
    d. if the people interact at more than a superficial level

23. Which of the following is an example of discrimination?
    a. thinking that women are less competent than men
    b. refusing to shop at a store owned and run by Asians
    c. believing that blacks are more athletic than whites
    d. disliking Iranians

24. Race is more potent than similarity of attitudes or values in determining our feelings and actions toward people when:
    a. social pressure is weak
    b. willingness to work with someone is the issue
    c. social pressure favors discrimination
    d. in all cases

25. Which of the following has a cooperative reward structure?
    a. a volleyball team
    b. a classroom where grades are assigned on a curve
    c. bidders at an auction
    d. two people sitting at opposite ends of a park each gazing at the stars

26. Research using the jigsaw method of teaching suggests that such a method results in:
    a. decreases in students' self-esteem
    b. increased liking for groupmates
    c. less cooperative attitudes
    d. poorer learning

27. The two general kinds of agreements that can be reached in a bargaining process are:
    a. competitive and interdependent agreements
    b. compromise and integrative agreement
    c. subordinate and superordinate agreements
    d. concessions and rejections

28. The GRIT approach to conflict resolution emphasizes:
    a. a gradual reduction in conflict while maintaining strength
    b. very large concessions in the early stages
    c. demands for reciprocation which, if not met, result in increased conflict
    d. waiting for the other side to make the first move

MULTIPLE CHOICE KEY

1. b	6. b	11. b	16. d	21. d	26. b
2. c	7. a	12. d	17. b	22. d	27. b
3. b	8. b	13. c	18. c	23. b	28. a
4. a	9. c	14. a	19. d	24. c	
5. d	10. b	15. d	20. a	25. a	

SHORT ANSWER ITEMS

1. Why is it necessary to adopt a cross-cultural perspective to social psychology?

2. Discuss how overlapping distributions and the inability to manipulate variables such as race, gender, or nationality make it difficult to interpret cross-cultural differences.

3. List and describe the six levels of analysis that Allport has applied to explain the occurrence of prejudice.

4. Describe social categorization and explain its importance.

5. Define and give an example of the three reward structures discussed in this chapter.

6. Under what conditions is intergroup contact likely to reduce conflict?

7. Describe five procedures for resolving conflicts.

APPLICATION QUESTIONS

1. Describe an instance of prejudice or discrimination that you are personally aware. What were the thoughts and feelings of those who displayed the prejudice or discrimination, and of those who were subject to it?

2. Think of a particular nationality, culture, religion, or ethnic group that you know something about, but aren't a member. Contrast your views about the characteristics of this group and of your group. How might ethnocentrism play a part in your beliefs.

3. Think of a time when you were engaged in intergroup conflict. Describe how the conflict influenced the communication and perceptions between you and the other person(s). How could one of the conflict reduction strategies discussed in this chapter be applied to this conflict?

CHAPTER FOURTEEN

SOCIAL BEHAVIOR IN THE PHYSICAL ENVIRONMENT

CHAPTER OUTLINE

Ambient Stress

- Temperature
- Noise
- Illumination
- Pollution

Privacy and Crowding

- Privacy Regulation
- Privacy in Open-Plan Offices
- Theories of Crowding
- Crowding and Residential Design

Spaces and Social Interaction

- Pleasant Places
- Seating Arrangements
- Proximity and Attraction

Attachment to Places

- Territories
- Homes
- Workplaces
- Neighborhoods

CHAPTER REVIEW

The physical environment is related to social behavior in a number of ways. The design of buildings, the ambient atmosphere, and the density of people, are among the aspects of the physical environment that affect social behavior. The perspective of environmental determinism suggests that the environment exerts a great deal of control on social behavior. However, the perspective of transactionalism suggests that there is mutual influence between the environment and social behavior. Thus, we not only conform to the environment, we also modify it.

The ambient environment includes temperature, sound, air quality and light. Exposure to unpleasant levels of these stimuli can produce arousal and even stress which, in turn, can affect our social behavior. In addition, stress can result in cognitive overload and a narrowing of attention. Reactions to environmental stimuli may vary with a person's adaptation level. Many ambient stressors make people more likely to respond aggressively when provoked. Ambient stressors such as unpleasant heat, or noxious odors may produce a negative reaction to outsiders. However, a shared stress effect may occur such that persons who are also sharing the stressful experience are liked.

Privacy involves the ability to regulate interpersonal interaction and to limit the accessibility of others. Privacy regulation is used to maintain an optimum level of social contact. A lack of privacy regulation can lead to problems. For example, persons who work in open-plan offices may suffer from a lack of privacy which sometimes results in worker dissatisfaction and poor performance on complex tasks.

Crowding involves excessive or unwanted social interactions that may result from being around too many people. Crowding is a subjective reaction which is not solely a result of the objective population density. The stress associated with crowding seems to result from factors such as cognitive overload, arousal, perceived lack of control, and lack of privacy regulation. In addition, crowding may produce withdrawal which can reduce one's social support network. Ironically, the presence of a large number of people may lessen social support.

Buildings with design features which allow for privacy regulation seem less crowded to the residents, and result in more positive social interaction. High density in prisons seems to lead to a variety of serious behavioral problems.

Pleasant settings tend to put people at ease, promote positive interpersonal interactions, and perhaps higher levels of performance. Sociopetal spaces allow people to maintain a comfortable distance and have eye contact; thus they are conducive to conversation. Seating patterns around a table affect patterns of conversation and are related to leadership. Physical proximity (propinquity) in housing, work space, and classroom seating is closely related to the development of friendships.

A territory is a place that we consider ours to occupy or control. Territories may include areas such as one's house, or work space, or temporary territories such as a seat at a library table. When a person leaves a temporary territory, he or she may mark it (perhaps by leaving a sweater or book bag) to show that the person has not finished using it. Individuals often personalize their homes, or workplaces. The concept of place identity suggests that persons often incorporate aspects of their environment (such as city person, apartment dweller, etc.) into their self-concept.

LEARNING OBJECTIVES

After completing Chapter 14, you should be able to:

1. Distinguish between environmental determinism and transactionalism. (p. 384)

2. Describe two factors which determine when stress is likely to be most disturbing. (p, 385)

3. Use the concepts of adaptation, adaptation level, and aftereffects to discuss reactions to stress. (p. 386)

4. Give four examples of ambient stressors. (p. 384-392)

5. Describe the relationships between ambient stressors such as temperature, pollution, and noise and aggression. (p. 387-391)

6. Explain the ways in which ambient stressors such as temperature and odor affect interpersonal liking. (p. 388-391)

7. Describe the importance of privacy regulation, and explain how a person might regulate privacy. (p. 392-393)

8. Describe 4 types of social spaces. (p. 393)

9. Describe open-plan offices, and explain the major advantages and disadvantages. (p. 393-394)

10. Distinguish between crowding and population density. (p. 394-395)

11. Explain the way in which social support determines the effects of crowding. (p. 395-396)

12. Describe differences in the behavior of students living in corridor and suite dormitories and relate these differences to privacy regulation. (p. 396-398)

13. Explain the difference between sociopetal and sociofugal spaces and describe how they affect behavior. (p. 400-401)

14. How is seating pattern related to behavior in a meeting?
(p. 401-402)

15. Describe the relationship between propinquity and interpersonal attraction and conflict. (p. 402-404)

16. Use the concept of place identity to explain territorial behavior (p. 404)

16. Describe the use of territorial markers. (p. 405-406)

17. Explain how place identity may affect one's satisfaction with his or her neighborhood. (408)

KEY TERMS

adaptation
adaptation level
ambient environment
ambient stressors
arousal

privacy
privacy regulation
private space
propinquity
public space

crowding
environmental determinism
homeworker
life space
narrowing of attention
neighborhood
noise
open-plan office
personalization
place identity
population density
semiprivate space
semipublic space
shared stress effect
sociofugal space
sociopetal space
status marker
stress
territorial marker
territory
transactionalism
work space

COMPLETION ITEMS

The view that features of the environment have a profound influence on behavior is called (1)_______________ _______________. Some feel that this view is overstated and adopt a less extreme view that we can mold our environment and alter our behavior; thus the environment has a more indirect effect. This view that there is mutual influence between people and the physical environment is called (2)_______________.

Temperature, noise, air quality and light are aspects of the (3)_______________ _______________. Unpleasant environmental conditions can produce arousal or even (4)_______________. People are able to show some (5)_______________ to stressful conditions such as constant noise or high temperatures. Thus, a Texan might easily tolerate the Texas summer while a visitor from Canada might find the heat stifling. The personal standard that a person develops based on experience is called an (6)_______________ _______________.

In general, ambient stressors are more disturbing if they are intense and (7)_______________. To cope with stress-induced cognitive overload, people under stress often exhibit a (8)_______________ _____ _______________. High temperature levels, air pollution, and loud, uncontrollable noise seem to (9)_______________ aggression. While uncomfortable ambient conditions will often increase negative interpersonal behavior, people who share the same stressful environment may like one another illustrating the (10)_______________ _______________ _______________.

Unwanted contact from others can result in a lack of (11)______________. In order to maintain the optimal level of social interaction, people engage in (12)______________-______________. Thus, we sometimes seek out social contact, and at other times avoid it. Various settings allow for differing amounts of privacy-regulation. Privacy-regulation is almost impossible in (13)______________ ______________ such as sidewalks and malls. Other places such as restaurants or office buildings allow for limited privacy regulation. Privacy-regulation is most complete in (14)______________ ______________ such as single bedrooms and private offices. The lack of a private workspace is sometimes a problem in (15)______________-______________ offices. (16)______________ ______________ is especially difficult in environments (like corridor-design dormitories) where (17)______________ spaces open directly onto public spaces.

The number of people per unit of space defines (18)______________ ______________. The subjective feeling of stress resulting from too much density is called (19)______________. A number of processes may be important causes of the negative effects of crowding. These include: arousal, cognitive overload, lack of control, lack of privacy regulation, and lack of social support. Because crowding may lead to withdrawal from others, it may result in reduced (20)______________ ______________. Residential designs which limit opportunities for (21)______________ ______________ seem more crowded and lead to social withdrawal and less positive social behavior.

Spaces which allow interaction at a comfortable distance and allow convenient eye contact are called (22)______________ spaces. Settings which discourage conversation are called (23)______________ ______________. Compared to classrooms with a semicircular seating pattern, traditional classrooms with rows of desks tend to (24)______________ classroom participation. Barriers such as desks can signal psychological (25)______________ between people. When seated around a table, persons are (26)______________ likely to talk to persons seated across from them (where eye contact is easy) than to someone seated to their side. Persons seated at the end of a rectangular meeting table are (27)______________ likely to be influential and perceived as leaders.

Research on proximity, or (28)______________, indicates that we often choose friends from those with nearby residences or work stations. Architectural features such as living on a cul-de-sac, or living near the apartment stairway also influence the formation of friendships.

Sometimes a person's self-concept will include thoughts about them and a particular place or type of setting. Thus, a person may think of himself or herself as a Bostonian, a suburbanite, or a person who lives on and loves the lake. These examples illustrate the concept of (29)______________-______________. Studies of satisfaction with one's current neighborhood illustrated the importance of a (30)______________ between a person's current residence and his or her (31)______________-______________.

A specific location that a person can control or use is called a (32)______________. Some (such as a house or private office) are controlled on a relatively permanent basis, while other territories are used on temporary basis (i.e., a phone booth). Using physical objects such as pictures, posters, and rugs to individualize one's room or other territory is called (33)______________. Persons may reserve a temporary territory (such as a place at a cafeteria table) by leaving territorial (34)______________ such as a notebook or a book bag. Objects, such as a private office or fancy furniture, may serve as (35)______________ ______________ and convey the person's social standing.

COMPLETION ITEM ANSWER KEY

(Answers printed in **bold type** require an exact match, but synonyms are acceptable for other items.)

1. **environmental determinism**
2. **transactionalism**
3. **ambient environment**
4. **stress**
5. **adaptation**
6. **adaptation level**
7. uncontrollable
8. **narrowing of attention**
9. increase
18. **population density**
19. **crowding**
20. **social support**
21. **privacy-regulation**
22. **sociopetal**
23. **sociofugal spaces**
24. discourage
25. distance
26. more
27. more

10. **shared stress effect**
11. **privacy**
12. **privacy-regulation**
13. **public spaces**
14. **private spaces**
15. **open-plan**
16. **privacy-regulation**
17. **private**
28. **propinquity**
29. **place-identity**
30. match
31. **place-identity**
32. **territory**
33. **personalization**
34. **markers**
35. **status markers**

MULTIPLE CHOICE ITEMS

1. The concept of adaptation level suggests that persons new to the city should experience the most crowding if they moved from:
   a. a larger city
   b. another part of the same city
   c. a high-rise apartment
   d. the country

2. Studies of crime rates in various cities suggest that aggression is more likely if:
   a. the temperature and humidity are high
   b. the victim is wearing red or is in a red car
   c. the aggressor has always lived in the city
   d. the victim is new to the city

3. The studies in which pedestrians passed novel objects such as a woman with a large teddy bear when traffic was noisy or quiet show that:
   a. noise reduces tendencies to act aggressively
   b. noise has more impact in cold weather
   c. noise lead to more negative evaluations of the objects
   d. noise can result in a narrowing of attention

4. Compared to those in comfortable rooms, persons in hot rooms who formed impressions of strangers from written descriptions of them:
   a. liked the stranger more
   b. liked the stranger less
   c. liked same sex strangers more and opposite sex strangers less
   d. liked same sex strangers less and opposite sex strangers more

5. Studies of air pollution suggest that:
   a. air pollution does not affect moods or performance
   b. air pollution has a temporary affect on moods and performance, but people quickly adapt
   c. air pollution has a negative affect on moods and performance, and people do not readily adapt to air pollution
   d. air pollution does not influence the extent of outdoor activity

6. People seem to talk more loudly if:
   a. light levels are high
   b. humidity is high
   c. someone is smoking
   d. they are in a pretty room

7. Which of the following is typically a sociofugal setting?
   a. a cozy den
   b. a cocktail lounge
   c. a restaurant
   d. an airport waiting area

8. When a group is seated at a rectangular table, the leader is likely to:
   a. stand
   b. sit along the side of the table
   c. sit at the end of the table
   d. avoid eye contact

9. Students are most likely to participate in classroom discussions if they sit:
   a. in the front center of the class
   b. in the middle of the class
   c. in the back of the class
   d. on the left side of the class

10. Festinger, Schacter, and Back's study of friendship in married student housing suggests that friendships were most likely to occur between:
   a. next door neighbors
   b. persons 2 or 3 doors away
   c. people in different buildings
   d. residents of well-decorated apartment buildings

11. The theory of __________ suggests that we try to maintain an optimum level of social contact:
    a. privacy regulation
    b. sociopetal spaces
    c. territorial dominance
    d. shared stress

12. Playgrounds, shopping malls, and sidewalks are examples of:
    a. status markers
    b. public spaces
    c. semiprivate spaces
    d. private places

13. Persons in open-plan offices report:
    a. more efficient work
    b. a lack of communication with colleagues
    c. less privacy
    d. increased creativity

14. College students living in dormitories who could not regulate their privacy:
    a. had more friends
    b. made better grades
    c. usually spent more time in their room
    d. were more likely to leave school for nonacademic reasons

15. Open-plan offices:
    a. interfere with normal communication
    b. are preferred by most workers
    c. lead to better performance on simple tasks, but poorer performance on complex tasks
    d. are very popular with college faculty

16. A person's private office would be an example of what kind of space?
    a. private
    b. secondary
    c. public
    d. interaction

17. Research by Sommer and others has indicated that, in public areas:
    a. markers can effectively protect space from intrusion
    b. people quickly invade marked territory
    c. it is virtually impossible to mark space effectively
    d. personal markers are usually stolen

18. Which of the following is an example of adaptation?
    a. You decide that you don't like your roommate's rock and roll music.
    b. The smell of garlic disturbs you.
    c. The heat has never bothered you.
    d. After living near an airport for awhile, you no longer notice the sound of planes.

19. Performance decrements on the part of subjects who had earlier experienced uncontrollable loud noise demonstrate:
    a. adaptation levels
    b. aftereffects
    c. privacy regulation
    d. territorial behavior

20. Crowding often leads to:
    a. increased social support
    b. decreased social support
    c. decreased arousal
    d. better privacy regulation

21. The effects of crowding are most severe if the crowding occurs in:
    a. residences or workplaces
    b. traffic
    c. parks and recreational areas
    d. public spaces

22. Student living in dormitories usually prefer:
    a. corridor dormitories
    b. suite dormitories
    c. high-rise dormitories
    d. noisy, active dormitories

23. Compared to residents of traditional corridor dormitories, residents of suite dormitories tend to:
    a. study less in the dorm
    b. spend less time in the dorm
    c. show less social withdrawal
    d. be more competitive

24. Studies show that high population density in prisons:
    a. leads to more pleasant social interaction
    b. results in greater social support
    c. makes privacy regulation easier
    d. results in many serious emotional and behavioral problems

25. A study of responses to others in environments unsuited to conversation (seats 11 feet apart) indicated that people:
    a. always try to rearrange the space to improve it
    b. seldom make attributions about others in such settings
    c. blame the discomfort on other people rather than the setting
    d. tend to speak faster

26. A cozy den which allows for easy talking and eye contact represents a:
    a. sociopetal space
    b. sociofugal space
    c. public space
    d. all of the above

27. Dimming the lights at a party might:
    a. cause people to feel more crowded
    b. cause people to be more concerned with the pollution caused by smokers
    c. cause people to talk more quietly
    d. cause people to be more concerned with the temperature

28. The theory that the physical environment has a powerful and decisive one-way influence on behavior is called:
    a. sociofugal space theory
    b. environmental determinism
    c. transactionalism
    d. privacy-regulation theory

MULTIPLE CHOICE ANSWER KEY

1. d	6. a	11. a	16. a	21. a	26. a
2. a	7. d	12. b	17. a	22. b	27. c
3. d	8. c	13. c	18. d	23. c	28. b
4. b	9. a	14. d	19. b	24. d	
5. c	10. a	15. c	20. b	25. c	

SHORT ANSWER ITEMS

1. Describe four features of the ambient environment. Give an example of how each one can affect social behavior.

2. Describe how seating arrangements can affect leadership and communication patterns.

3. Describe how dormitory design can affect behavior. Why does dormitory design have such effects?

4. Explain why ambient stressors sometimes lead to greater liking for others and sometimes lead to less liking.

APPLICATION QUESTIONS

1. Describe a situation in which some aspect of the ambient environment affected social behavior.

2. Describe a specific sociopetal space and a specific sociofugal space that you know. Compare and contrast the two spaces.

3. Describe a time when you felt crowded. Discuss the incident in terms of at least two of the following concepts: arousal, cognitive overload, perceived control, privacy regulation, social support.

4. Describe one of your primary, secondary, and public territories.